WITHDRAWN

Southern Literary Studies
Louis D. Rubin, Jr., Editor

The
Southern
Vision of
Andrew Lytle

The
Southern
Vision of
Andrew Lytle

MARK LUCAS

Louisiana State University Press
Baton Rouge and London

Designer: Christopher Wilcox
Typeface: ITC Garamond Book
Typesetter: G&S Typesetters, Inc.
Printer: Thomson-Shore, Inc.
Binder: John Dekker and Sons, Inc.

10 9 8 7 6 5 4 3 2 1

The author gratefully acknowledges Andrew Lytle for permission to quote from his works; Helen Ransom Forman for permission to quote from a letter of John Crowe Ransom to Andrew Lytle, dated December 11, 1925; Helen H. Tate for permission to quote from letters of Allen Tate to Andrew Lytle, dated March 15, 1927, April 1, 1929, July 31, 1929, and June 9, 1930; and Nancy Tate Wood for permission to quote from a letter of Caroline Gordon to Andrew Lytle, dated March 15, 1943.

Extracts from the letters of Andrew Lytle are published with the permission of Princeton University Library; Special Collections, The Jean and Alexander Heard Library, Vanderbilt University; and Andrew Lytle.

The extracts from letters of Donald Davidson to Andrew Lytle, dated June 11, 1929, and February 3, 1930, are published with the permission of Special Collections, The Jean and Alexander Heard Library, Vanderbilt University.

Publication of this book has been assisted by a grant from the Andrew W. Mellon Foundation.

Library of Congress Cataloging-in-Publication Data

Lucas, Mark, 1953–
    The southern vision of Andrew Lytle.

    (Southern literary studies)
    Bibliography: p.
    Includes index.
    1. Lytle, Andrew Nelson, 1902–   —Criticism and
interpretation.   2. Southern States in literature.
3. Southern States—Historiography.   I. Title.
II. Series.
PS3523.Y88Z74   1986   813'.52   86–21076
ISBN 0–8071–1338–7

To
my mother and father

Contents

Preface and Acknowledgments

Andrew Nelson Lytle grew up with this double image before him: a girl shot in the neck by a Yankee sniper, her shoes filling with blood; an old woman wearing a ribbon to hide the scar. It was his grandmother. He dedicated *Bedford Forrest and His Critter Company* to her, and in so doing, he honored someone who had actually heard the wild yell of Forrest's riders as they raised the dust of Rutherford County turnpikes. That those hoof-beats still echoed some seventy years later in the mind of her grandson suggests something of why the word *southern* is part of the title of this study.

Lytle's grandmother Nelson is an apt symbol of the South into which he was born, in Murfreesboro, Tennessee, on December 2, 1902. His parents, Robert Logan Lytle and Lillie Belle Nelson, were both from established Tennessee families, Murfreesboro itself having been founded on land donated by a Lytle forebear. As *A Wake for the Living* attests, young Andrew's upbringing in Murfreesboro and northern Alabama took place within a thick network of family connections, and the world of his and his sister's childhood was marked by a deep sense of community. Robert Lytle, a landowner involved in cotton farming and timber production, was a celebrated raconteur and repository of family lore who helped keep the southern past vividly alive for his son. After secondary school at Sewanee Military Academy, Lytle spent a year of tutored study in France. He was about to matriculate at Oxford University when he was called home to Tennessee by the death of his grandfather. He enrolled at Vanderbilt University instead, and it was a very good time to *be* at Vanderbilt. He was a friend of fellow undergraduate Robert Penn Warren and the student of two other men later to become, like Warren, his Agrarian compatriots—John Crowe Ransom and Donald Davidson. Lytle published one poem in the *Fugitive* but was not a formal member of the remarkable group of poets that met fortnightly and produced the magazine; play writing, not poetry or fiction, was his growing literary interest in those years. After graduating from Vanderbilt in 1925, he managed his father's cotton farm for a year. He then left the South for two years of graduate work under George Pierce Baker at the Yale School of Drama and some seasons of professional acting in New York. This period spent out of the South clarified and intensified his sense of himself as a southerner, and when he went back to the South in 1929, he went back to stay.

It is with the intensification of Lytle's southern identity, in the late 1920s, that this study begins. The first three chapters discuss the writing of *Bedford Forrest and His Critter Company* as Lytle's accession to a tradition, and then examine his involvement in the Agrarian enterprise and its publications, from *I'll Take My Stand* through *Who Owns America?* The next six chapters explore Lytle's literary imagination vis-à-vis the Agrarian enterprise and the South in general. How Lytle handled the shift in his career from polemical to fictional expression—from southern Agrarianism to southern fiction—is the subject of Chapter IV, which focuses on his best-known short story, "Jericho, Jericho, Jericho." Chapter V is a discussion of *The Long Night* and the dense social texture of Lytle's fictional world, while Chapter VI analyzes *At the Moon's Inn,* focusing on the book's symbolic depiction of the spiritual decline of the West and on the southern roots of that theme. *A Name for Evil,* Chapter VII argues, has an interesting relationship to events in Lytle's life during the period of its composition and demonstrates a rich complexity in his view of the past. Chapter VIII's commentary on *The Velvet Horn,* Lytle's most important work, looks at the intricate layering in this novel's portrayal of the South at a pivotal moment—the present against the background of the past, history against the background of myth, time against the background of eternity. The concluding chapter examines Lytle's book of family memoirs, *A Wake for the Living,* both as a glimpse of the circumstances of time and place that made him an artist and as a late-career coda for central Agrarian themes.

These themes, Lytle's southern *pietas,* are those of a man intensely aware of the currents of time and change in his culture. The South's shift in his time from an agrarian to an urban-industrial society left him disquietedly astraddle the old and the new, and his essay for *I'll Take My Stand* first articulated this disquiet. Beyond the realm of polemics, however, he molded a career as an artist out of the complexities of self-definition in such circumstances. I have tried to illuminate these complexities while providing introductory readings of the major works. What is the relationship between Lytle's work and the time and place from which it grew? Of the many questions that still confront the scholar of Lytle's craggy muse, this is the central one addressed herein.

Because of much help and kindness along the way, my labors have been pleasures. A few words of gratitude here can hardly be sufficient, but they are at least a start.

To Mr. Lytle himself I am deeply indebted, not only for allowing me to see and quote from his papers but also for patiently enduring my questions. The incomparable hospitality of the Log Cabin is a name for the rich horn and the spreading laurel tree.

To my mentors and colleagues at Centre College I owe much. One and all, they are the furthest thing imaginable from the sad scholar who (Lytle's Jack Cropleigh speaking) "put out his eyes reading footnotes, and when he was called on to recite, cried,—The text, oh, where, Jesus, is the text?" In matters great and small they have been my support. I offer thanks, then, to Carol Bastian, Paul Cantrell, Charles Hazelrigg, Milton Reigelman, Mary Sweeney, and Roberta White. Grateful acknowledgments are in order, also, for two summer-study grants from Centre. My thanks in particular go to the Faculty Development Committee and to Dean Leonard DiLillo. And to Her Infallibility Patsy McAfee my appreciation goes for the best of all typing.

Three libraries made my researches possible: the Princeton University Library, Vanderbilt's Jean and Alexander Heard Library, and the Grace Doherty Library of Centre College. I am beholden to the Special-Collections staffs at Vanderbilt and Princeton for their efficiency and for their permission to quote from unpublished material. For timely acquisitions, tireless interlibrary loan efforts, and many other helps, I am grateful to Stan Campbell, Susanne McCollough, Bob Glass, Nancy Knight, and the entire Doherty staff.

For providing challenge, advice, and encouragement at an early juncture I should like to thank Robert Bain, George Lensing, Townsend Ludington, and J. R. Raper. Also not forgotten is the special support, early and late, of Dan Lucas and Steve Powell. And to Louis D. Rubin, Jr., under whose tutelage I first started down this road, I owe a debt of gratitude not only for the blunt wisdom of his counsel (I should have listened better) but even more for the inspiration of his example.

Last and most, my thanks go to my children, for their patience; to my parents, for their faith; and to my wife, for everything. The most of what I owe her must here go unspoken, but not unfelt.

The
Southern
Vision of
Andrew Lytle

Bedford Forrest
and the Southern Inheritance

"Humh! De Gin'ral's hoss show is gittin' poe."
"What do you mean, Georgiana? That horse can't lose weight. It's bronze."
"Well'm, I seen 'em when dey put him up dar, and I see him now—and he
show is poe."
"How in the world could that happen, Georgiana?"
"I don't know'm. I regon de Gin'ral must ride him of a night."

—*Bedford Forrest and
His Critter Company*

If the rebellious spirit of General Forrest, late of the Confederate
States of America, lived on when the above passage appeared in
1931, it most certainly lived on in Andrew Nelson Lytle, the
young firebrand among the southern Agrarians. Championing
Forrest as a heroic symbol of the Old South, Lytle approached his
subject with none of the cool reserve of the academic biographer; he wrote not only in memoriam but also in defense. Importantly, *Bedford Forrest and His Critter Company* represents
Lytle's accession to a tradition, and as such the book is significant
not as a military biography but as a preliminary step in Lytle's
Agrarian rebuke to—in his eyes—the modern juggernaut called

Progress.[1] Lytle's first book was indeed a decisive event in his genesis as an artist, for it gave him his special focus on the modern world and afforded him the chance to study upland southern society through the time of its Civil War destruction—the very society that forms the fictional milieu of a great part of his work. That in the late 1920s Lytle felt his tradition to be in need of reclamation, though, merits comment before I go on to look at the particular image of the Old South portrayed in *Bedford Forrest.*

In the years immediately following World War I, the South began to feel it was "back in the Union," to use Lytle's phrase for what many have expressed. After half a century of poverty, there was folding money in the South again and a pervasive acceptance of New South materialism. Furthermore, the young southerner coming of age in these years was all too likely, as Lytle recounted in 1936, to be "ignorant of Southern history and what its cultural tradition had to offer the arts." [2] The reasons for this included the ahistorical temper of the New South attitude and the fact that official American history was cut to a New England pattern. ("Whoever wins an internecine war," Lytle has said, "writes the history of that war. And the textbooks as well.") [3] Most important was probably youth's natural fixation on the present; however, an incident soon arose that helped to jolt some of the brightest young southerners, Lytle among them, out of the mere present.

The Scopes evolution trial, now famous as the Monkey trial,

1. A note on chronology: Letters make clear that Lytle was in the midst of the manuscript of *Bedford Forrest* when, in the summer of 1930, he wrote "The Hind Tit" for *I'll Take My Stand.* For this reason it serves my purpose to examine the place of *Bedford Forrest* in Lytle's career first, before turning to "The Hind Tit" and its sister essays among Lytle's polemics.

2. Andrew Lytle, "They Took Their Stand: The Agrarian View After Fifty Years," *Modern Age,* XXIV (1980), 115, and "The Approach of the Southern Writer to His Material," Atlanta *Constitution,* November 29, 1936, Book Sec., 14. There was, however, no shortage of that anecdotal kind of history that was retailed around the hearth fire and became part of the southern youth's consciousness.

3. Lytle, "They Took Their Stand," 115.

2

began in Dayton, Tennessee, the summer after Lytle's graduation from Vanderbilt University in 1925. The case involved the prosecution of a schoolteacher for breaking a state law banning the theory of evolution from public classrooms. Speaking for the state, William Jennings Bryan based his argument on a fallacious biblical literalism. Clarence Darrow, head lawyer for the defense, made Bryan look ridiculous while H. L. Mencken, head publicist for the defense, made the whole South look ridiculous. He and his fellow northern journalists sent home reams of lively copy portraying the rural South as little more than a land of half-wits and snakehandlers. Bryan, in Mencken's eyes, epitomized the rural southerner; to wit, "a poor clod . . . deluded by childish theology, full of an almost pathological hatred of all learning, all human dignity, all fine and noble things." [4]

Meanwhile, young Lytle, a rural southerner himself, was running the family cotton farm in north Alabama, and though no fundamentalist, he was not disposed to take kindly to Mencken's scattershot condemnation of the rural South. Nor was he alone, for the two men he had respected most while a student at Vanderbilt—philosophy professor Herbert Sanborn and English professor John Crowe Ransom—began to question the glib assumptions of the Mencken crew, a fact that bolstered Lytle's own instinctive protest. [5] Sanborn, a Munich-educated New Englander, immediately saw through the zoolike atmosphere to a fundamental clash below the surface—a secular religion based on belief in science versus a spiritual religion based on faith in the Bible. Ransom, too, felt that the issue was not nearly so simple as the urban sophisticates were painting it, and though he did not go public with his distaste for scientific liberalism for several years, he applauded Sanborn for "coming out strong in the newspapers against the evolutionists and the Modernists." Lytle himself came to see the northern diatribes as meant not only to make the South "laughable as backward and ignorant" but also to

4. H. L. Mencken, *Prejudices: Fifth Series* (New York, 1926), 68.
5. Author's interview with Andrew Lytle, March 6, 1980. Lytle studied Aristotelian logic under Sanborn and creative writing under Ransom.

have the "more insidious" aim of "a forced acceptance of belief in a secular instead of a divine order of the universe."[6]

Everything in Lytle's small-town Tennessee upbringing told him that the southern community was not the debased thing being held up for the nation to scorn, and he felt sharply the South's virtual prostration before the forces of scientism. Consequently, he believed that now was the time to deepen his awareness of the southern community and its roots, for a first step in countering the attacks of "the Modernists" was to connect the rural southerner with a proud tradition. Thus, with the eminent historian Frank Owsley as friend and guide, Lytle began a seven-year probe of his region's heritage—a probe that produced the Forrest biography, yielded essays on John Calhoun, Robert E. Lee, John Taylor, and the southern plain folk, and in the end bore fruit in the four novels.[7]

All of this helps to explain the otherwise perplexing question, Why would a young actor from the provinces who had just made it onto the New York stage begin spending his few leisure hours poring over dusty military annals? The answer certainly has something to do with the fact that the young actor was from Tennessee and, beyond this, that he was not *in* Tennessee just then but in his nation's literary capital, the symbol of the prevailing culture of America—New York City.

Lytle has written that despite the literary awakening of the South in the 1920s a would-be dramatist from Tennessee was not likely to find a literary center near home to nurture him. Such a man "was forced to flee to New York."[8] When Lytle graduated from Vanderbilt in 1925, he was bent on a life in the theater, and after one year of running his father's farm, he went for training as a playwright to George Pierce Baker's school of drama at Yale University. Baker's good advice to Lytle was to use his cultural background to write about southern people in southern settings.

6. John Crowe Ransom to Andrew Lytle, December 11, 1925, in Andrew Lytle Papers, Special Collections, The Jean and Alexander Heard Library, Vanderbilt University; Lytle, "They Took Their Stand," 116.

7. Lytle, "They Took Their Stand," 116

8. Lytle, "The Approach of the Southern Writer," 14.

Unfortunately, when the fledgling playwright left academe late in 1928 to prove himself in New York, he found the city to have some crucial defects both as a place to live and as a literary capital.

For one thing, he learned to his confusion that as a playwright "he must disavow or satirize anything that was particularly Southern." What this amounted to was a form of provincialism on the part of the New York theater, because, in Lytle's view, it demanded that a writer "cut himself off from his place of nativity and become a New Yorker." Instead of "the head where all is made articulate," New York was "a head without a body," connected to other regions by economic concerns only. Caught in this dilemma, Lytle pondered whether "to give in to the colonial state of mind and write what New York wanted to hear about the South, or to cease writing altogether." By turning to the southern past, however, he both voiced a protest and began to make for himself the cultural sustenance New York could not supply. It was not until he began to research the life of Forrest that he "became aware of the richness of this tradition and its possibilities."[9]

Further, New York life seemed frenetic, impersonal, and cash-mad in ways hard for someone from the traditional community of Murfreesboro to fathom or excuse. "I am writing to learn how the winter has gone with you," Lytle wrote to Donald Davidson at Vanderbilt, "and to tell you that this barbaric city is no place for a Christian to spend too much time in."[10] The urban-industrial society, fragmented, deracinated, and hectic, was a shock to the sensibilities of someone raised in a largely agrarian society that—because of the cultural lag occasioned by the South's military defeat and then its isolation—still had fixed and leisurely patterns of community behavior, which tended to prevent its citizens from becoming too busy with making a living to make a life. There were many things wrong with the South, but when Lytle looked there from the vantage point of New York, even

9. *Ibid.*

10. Andrew Lytle to Donald Davidson, February 21, 1929, in Donald Davidson Papers, Special Collections, The Jean and Alexander Heard Library, Vanderbilt University.

some of its defects (relative poverty, for instance) looked like virtues. Metropolitan life was an object lesson for Lytle in how different he was in manners and attitudes, and the experience of difference threw those formerly unconscious manners and attitudes into a new light, making them more important. That is, living in New York intensified his southern identity—a familiar paradox. Thus, in the midst of a bewildering city seemingly hostile to the honest impulses of his imagination, Lytle could turn to Forrest and the antebellum South as images of a life to be reaffirmed.

As it happened, another southerner in New York City—Allen Tate—had already undergone the same intensification of southern identity. Lytle had been good friends with Robert Penn Warren at Vanderbilt but had not known Tate. Both Tate and Lytle, however, had been favorites of their teacher and friend John Crowe Ransom, who eventually pulled the strings to bring the two wandering southerners together. At Ransom's suggestion, Tate wrote to Lytle at Yale, on March 15, 1927: "I should be very happy to have you call upon us here the next time you are in New York. . . . Interesting things are, I believe, at last stirring in the South, and in that part of the South which we cannot help taking about with us forever, wherever we may go." Lytle took up the invitation before the spring was over and went calling at Tate's basement apartment in Greenwich Village. In a matter of moments, the two fell to discussing the Monkey trial in Tennessee "as a liberal attack on our traditional inheritance." [11] They were sure to have talked about Tate's latest project as well, a biography of Stonewall Jackson (published in 1928).

Thus was a lifelong friendship begun. With Tate's help Lytle soon made an agreement with a publisher, and by the next year Lytle was at work on a Civil War biography of his own. [12] The friends' deep interest in southern history prompted a tour of

11. Allen Tate to Andrew Lytle, March 15, 1927, in Lytle Papers; Lytle, "They Took Their Stand," 116.

12. Author's interview with Lytle, March 6, 1980. Tate's publishers asked Lytle to produce half of a Forrest biography first, for their inspection. If they thought the manuscript good enough, they would pay Lytle an advance and publish the

Civil War battlefields in the summer of 1928, when Lytle and the Tates "travelled in a second-hand Ford from New York to Alabama." Lytle later continued the pilgrimage alone, retracing Forrest's maneuvers through Tennessee and Mississippi, and confronting history as directly as possible through diaries, letters, battle reports, and, especially, the old people—all the surviving veterans of Forrest's cavalry whom he could find, as well as those, like his grandmother Nelson, "who [had] heard on the hard turn-pike the sudden beat of his horses' hoofs and the wild yell of his riders." [13]

"Out of my great admiration and love for this remarkable man," Lytle wrote to Donald Davidson in 1929, "I have set myself to doing a biography of General Nathan Bedford Forrest, than which there was no better military commander in the West." [14] This remarkable man was the Memphis slave trader-*cum*-cavalry gallant of whom General Sherman once declared, "There will never be peace in Tennessee until Forrest is dead!" (305). Legendary for his 1864 raid on Union headquarters in Memphis, when the Federal commander ran away in his underwear while the Rebels rode off with his uniform, Forrest distinguished himself in other, more substantial ways as well. A description of his victory at Brice's Cross-Roads, accomplished by dismounting his men to fight as infantry in a double envelopment, was later used as the text for a lecture by Marshal Foch (304).

Part of Lytle's thesis, which Shelby Foote has more recently seconded, is that the war zone west of the Appalachians was crucial, a belief that emphasizes the potential importance of Forrest. As Lytle says: "The magnificent Lee and the invincible Jackson were to wage such war in Virginia that history would come to ignore the importance of western battles. But it was there that

---

completed work. It was to be (and became) part of Minton/Balch's Civil War series.

13. Lytle, "They Took Their Stand," 119, and *Bedford Forrest and His Critter Company* (New York, 1931), v, hereinafter cited parenthetically by page number in the text.

14. Lytle to Davidson, February 21, 1929, in Davidson Papers.

the war must be won and lost, for the heart of the Confederacy lay in the lower South, between the mountains and the Mississippi River. To lose Tennessee permanently was to lose the cause, since Tennessee was the strategic center of the whole defense" (88). The principals in this theatre of war, according to Lytle, were Jefferson Davis, Braxton Bragg, Joseph E. Johnston, and Forrest. Considerably more than a raid-and-run partisan, Forrest could have been the savior of the South, Lytle argues, had he not been underestimated by Davis and undercut by Bragg. "In the role of Aegisthus," Bragg was the villain, for not until he "cast his shadow across the stage did the drama about to be played assume definitely its tragic form. He was the shadow, the element, that complicated the plot. All the strength of the other three, instead of gathering to fall in unison upon the enemy, became lost in the toils which gathered upon his entrance" (88).

Bragg was timid, bureaucratic, and theoretical in his approach to war—the antithesis of Forrest. Central to Lytle's admiration of Forrest is the Confederate cavalry hero's alleged wilderness-born realism. Unlike Jefferson Davis, Forrest saw the great conflict for what it was—total war—and was willing to act on this knowledge. Sentimental chivalry and restricted war, Lytle emphasizes, were empty forms to Forrest, who saw the issue at hand without fear, self-doubt, or overrefinement. And at bottom, the issue, in Lytle's as well as Forrest's eyes, was nothing less than freedom or death.

Such clearsightedness, Lytle contends, was the result of Forrest's background, the particular form of southern society from which he came. Indeed, Lytle underscores Forrest's wilderness upbringing even to the point of inventing dialogue for a story about young Bedford night stalking a panther in the Chickasaw country of north Mississippi. The boy gets his panther, refusing to abide by any sporting code along the way, for, he observes, "The way of the wilderness was to kill or to be killed" (7). Later, in an unnatural but equally absolute contest, Forrest was to say, while sharpening an ornamental sword, "War means fighting, and fighting means killing" (139). Lytle records these words with relish, in admiration for the plain man's superior insight. No cotton snob, no ineffectual idealist, and certainly no modern, Lytle's Forrest was a man with a sense of direction, who summed up all that was best in his class, the southern yeomanry.

This class, the "plain folk," was the largest group of people in the antebellum South, comprising at least four million largely nonslaveholding whites who were not part of the plantation economy. Neither rich nor destitute, these self-sufficient country people usually owned the land they tilled, concentrating on food crops rather than money crops.[15] In myth they have come to be identified with those hookworm-ridden, malarial creatures called "poor white trash," but part of Lytle's purpose is to dispel the myth.

The southern yeomen, Lytle explains, "were going out to fight because they had heard the Yankees were coming down to tromp their fields and tear up their barns" (36). The "freest people in the South," they were marching out of the up-country, off the borders of the plantations, and away from the newly settled states "to defend their particular way of life" (36). Lytle asserts that in view of the yeomanry's fiercely guarded independence and sheer numbers, Jefferson Davis's single greatest mistake was "to rest the foundations of the Confederacy on cotton and not on the plain people" (36).[16]

Setting the record straight on the yeomanry is certainly a valid objective, and Lytle's excoriation of Davis derives from feelings deeper than an armchair Confederate's desire to refight the war and show how the South might have won. Further, one suspects an element of playful brio behind Lytle's waving of the Stars and Bars. The exuberance, however, contributes to the book's shortcoming as a biography: the one-dimensionality of its portrayal of Forrest. For instance, Lytle writes straight apologia for Forrest's role as first grand wizard of the Ku Klux Klan ("the last brilliant example in Western Culture of what Feudalism could do") rather

15. See the book later published by Lytle's compatriot in these matters, Frank Lawrence Owsley: *Plain Folk of the Old South* (Baton Rouge, 1949).

16. Lytle drags Jefferson Davis over the same coals Allen Tate does in Tate's *Jefferson Davis, His Rise and Fall* (New York, 1929). Lytle acknowledges his indebtedness to Tate in a bibliographical note (*Bedford Forrest,* 394).

than going behind the issue of cultural defense to probe the seeming absolutism and guiltlessness of Forrest's mind (384). Thus, ostensible complexities in the character of Forrest go unplumbed so that "a son of the gods" can emerge in unshadowed heroism (68).

Perhaps it is not fair to ask of Lytle the biographer what Lytle the novelist teaches us to expect: that reality is always more complex than any neat explanation can account for. At any rate, Lytle certainly followed the then official southern view of Reconstruction represented by the work of such a respected scholar as Walter Lynwood Fleming, who approved of the early KKK for bringing order to the social chaos between 1866 and 1870. (One might add that the northern historian Claude Bowers had recently affirmed essentially the same view as well.) Whether deficient as speculative history or not, Lytle's interpretation of the Klan's first years was, in 1931, competent scholarship. Further, it is well to remember that Lytle was born into the shards of an older society whose form was still visible in his youth and whose caste system was part of a centuries-old way of life. To be morally indignant with Lytle for his not being morally indignant with Forrest is, in a sense, anachronistic, a failure to see Lytle in his time and place.[17]

In any event, the significant thing is not that the biography may be too unremittingly cast in the high heroic mode but that Lytle wrote it at all, thereby retrieving, in a sense, his ancestral inheritance. Moreover, there are hints of the embryonic novelist in *Bedford Forrest*. For instance, Lytle goes beyond the scientific historian's just-facts exposition to include the telling detail: the white beard of foam on the chin of the hard-ridden horse, a July so parched that the gnats swarm to drink the riders' sweat, the blood-soaked crackers in the haversack of a dead comrade, the stray hog among the amputated limbs. And Lytle does not hesi-

17. On this matter, Richard King's scorn of the book is overly simple. See *A Southern Renaissance: The Cultural Awakening of the American South, 1930–1955* (New York, 1980), 57–58.

10

tate to use a well-turned anecdote to capture the spirit of a scene. An old woman, for instance, complains that "Mr. Forrest and his hoss critters formed a streak of fight in my back yard, tore down my fence, and plumb ruint my ash-hopper" (127). And a green recruit at Chickamauga, "when his whole line dropped to reload, looked around him in wonder and said, 'Great God, the first shot and got 'em all but me!'" (217). All the same, the imaginative details and the anecdotes do not by themselves augur the complexity of the man who would later write *At the Moon's Inn* and *The Velvet Horn.*

Indeed, there may be danger of making too much of *Bedford Forrest,* but however minor the biography is when measured against Lytle's later achievement, it bears importance as Lytle's accession to his southern inheritance. This taking up of an inheritance gave him a special point of view on a contemporary situation that he saw all too rapidly descending into the vortex of scientism and industrialism. Particularly relevant to this point of view are the biography's redactions of the antebellum good life and the meaning of the Civil War.

Readers of Lytle's fiction and polemics immediately note that his image of the good life centers not on Tidewater or Deep South plantation society, but on the folk culture of the upland South. In view of this it is significant that of all the Confederates— Robert E. Lee, for instance—who might have satisfied Lytle's early penchant for hero worship, he settled on the Tennessean Bedford Forrest. Forrest was the hero of *Lytle's* South, the up-country region west of the mountains; thus, in an oblique way the biography held an element of self-definition for Lytle. The First Families of Virginia tradition was not a part of Lytle's heritage or psychology, as it was in some ways for Tate. Rather, Lytle's great-great-grandfather had left for Tennessee from the same county in the "yeoman state" of North Carolina that Forrest's grandfather had set out from. In fact, throughout *Bedford Forrest* Lytle, like Forrest, shows a certain impatience with the Virginia squires "who fashioned their ways after the English gentry of the eighteenth century" (9). Further, he points out that in the old

Southwest the only difference between the plain folk and the cotton snobs was that of one or two generations and that "the rich snobs were ashamed of their pioneer ancestry" (36).

Clearly the plain folk are part of Lytle's image of an admirable social and moral ethic in his region's past. Indeed, Davis's basic problem, according to Lytle, was that he "forgot he was born in a dog-run . . . and that the backbone of the South and its armies was the plain people" (356). Forrest, however, did not forget. The quintessential representative of yeoman stock, he "emerged from the cabin" to establish himself "as a strong man of his Culture," with the plain man's individualism, hardihood, and common sense to recommend him (390). With no prior military training, Forrest rose from the ranks to be commander of a division. Over and over he faced and defeated West Point–trained officers who lacked his concrete knowledge of land, horses, men, and nature. As Forrest himself characteristically observed, "Whenever I met one of them fellows who fit by note, I generally whipped hell out of him before he pitched the tune" (256). Even Forrest's earthy talk exemplified what Lytle values in the plain folk—an unpretentious, rural wisdom that rises above mere refinement.

His fighting "as heartening as sow-belly and corn bread," Forrest was someone the southern plain folk could rally behind (102). He possessed the power to galvanize his men into unity, to give them "the feeling that the South was one big clan, fighting that the small man, as well as the powerful, might live as he pleased" (149). Importantly, the freedom that the antebellum plain man was so ready to defend, says Lytle, was a function of Jeffersonian democracy. Those who "hired out to factory masters . . . became dependent on the will of another," but the southern plain man was "beholden to no other" because he could provide all his family's necessities through his own labors (10).[18] Nor was he sentenced to a life of pleasureless toil, as

18. Slavery complicates the issue of antebellum democracy. On this head, Lytle must resort to speaking of a benevolent "southern feudalism" in which the slave "owned the master as much as the master owned him" (27).

vignettes of old-time feasts and dances in *Bedford Forrest* make clear. Even amidst the hardships of 1863, for instance, the Tennesseans could enjoy the amenities of the folkways they treasured.

> The ladies had been as busy as the men. Fires on the kitchen hearths had been going at full blast. The kettles sizzled, the ovens filled with cake batter were set in the ashes and covered with hot coals; the whites of eggs foamed; red whiskey poured into the yolks and cooked them for the nog. By evening all was ready. The square was lighted by bonfires and pine torches. The courthouse had been cleared, the candles lit.
>
> The fiddles were tuned, the bows drawn across the strings, and a loud vibrant voice called the partners to their places. Some treaded the Virginia reel; others treaded through the mazes of a quartet, but most every trooper favored the square dance. The fiddles whined, the prompter called the figgers, the floor shook, and the booted feet swung corners, set to partners, circled to the left, until the east was gray with dawn. (251)

In the self-reliance and folk culture of the plain man, Lytle sees the outlines of an image of the Old South that embodies a silent reproach to modern New York and points toward the Agrarianism of "The Hind Tit." In broadest terms, the southern way of life Lytle reveres was a rich synthesis of two cultural strains, the "static, historical, cultural" European strain and the "dynamic, revolutionary, imperial" pioneer strain (15).[19] A vigorous agrarian culture tempered by a formal grace is Lytle's broad conception of the Old South.

However, across this way of life soon fell the shadow of northern venality. Lytle's partisan explanation of the Civil War portrays the conflict in terms of a clash between antithetical cultures. The South, "a people living almost entirely on the land," was forced to face off against the North, "a people loyal to a commercial and fast-growing industrialism which demanded that the duty of the

---

19. As the Tate-Lytle correspondence shows, this idea of two cultural strains accounts for Lytle's belief that Forrest was a "Southern American," whereas Robert E. Lee, a member of the Virginia gentry, was essentially "European." See, for instance, Tate to Lytle, April 1, 1929, in Lytle Papers.

citizen must not be life, liberty, and the pursuit of happiness but a willing consumption of the produce of Northern manufacture" (31). The Radical Republicans, Lytle contends, brayed about slavery chiefly in a cynical effort to pervert the Constitution, destroy the old equilibrium between plow and factory, and extend the industrial dispensation. Finally, when the North had won—primarily because of the idealism of Davis and the stupidity of Bragg, and decidedly not because of any natural superiority in industrialism—Republican Reconstruction "aimed at complete destruction of the Southern States" in order to prevent the reassembling of the old political union (381).

Controversial as Lytle's interpretation of the Civil War may be, it would prove important to the rest of his career as a writer. The war Lytle pictures was no simple matter of the Lord's appointed "trampling out the vintage where the grapes of wrath are stored." Rather, it had more to do with the mercenary desires of northern industrialism. That to some degree Lytle was delineating the Old South in ideal form was part of the strategy; a reconstituted image of history could foster a clear-eyed attitude toward dire modern conditions. Not one merely to brood on the past, Lytle was more than ready, as Tate remarked, to "*use* the past for daring and *positive* ends." [20] That Lytle's next project was his essay for *I'll Take My Stand* is no surprise.

Forrest's name, which had never known defeat, became in afteryears a "spiritual comforter to the people of the Southwest" (390). In the modern context of the swift surge past the Mason-Dixon line of urbanization, industrialization, and mechanization, however, Lytle's invocation of Forrest as "the most typical strong man of the Agrarian South" is less in the spirit of comfort than of renewed fight (393). Forrest! thou shouldst be living at this hour—it is not altogether fanciful to read this between the lines, though Lytle and his fellow Agrarian "Generals," as they sometimes addressed one another, were certainly not waiting for the dead to take action. Lytle surely qualified as the "unreconstructed

20. Tate to Lytle, July 31, 1929, in Lytle Papers.

Southerner" Ransom described in *I'll Take My Stand,* for "his regard for a certain terrain, a certain history, and a certain inherited way of living" is the very stuff of which *Bedford Forrest* is
made.[21] And his soil, history, and inheritance, Lytle began to see,
embodied an antidote to the urban materialism that held the
field after the Civil War and was now coarsening American life.

21. John Crowe Ransom, "Reconstructed but Unregenerate," in *I'll Take My
Stand: The South and the Agrarian Tradition* (1930; rpr. Baton Rouge, 1977), 1.

15

II

Using the Inheritance
"The Hind Tit" and Agrarianism

In taking up the Forrest biography, Lytle had claimed and to some degree codified his inheritance as a southerner. The next step was using that inheritance in an offensive against modern disorder. Lytle resented the northern ridicule occasioned by the Scopes trial, regarded the mode of life in New York City as alien, and generally felt ill at ease as a southerner in the Age of Coolidge. He wanted to *do* something, and for him, to act was to write. He therefore wrote the Agrarian essay "The Hind Tit" for *I'll Take My Stand: The South and the Agrarian Tradition.* "The Hind Tit" is both a pastoral exaggeration of the good life on the land and an impassioned rebuke to the urban-industrial view of God, man, and the state.

Aside from the ringleaders of the Agrarian enterprise—Davidson, Tate, and Ransom—Lytle was probably more deeply involved in the movement than anyone else. The intensity of his identification with the cause, a running motif in correspondence from this period, is a good example of the remarkable cohesiveness at this time of men strikingly independent in character, a cohesiveness catalyzed by one crucial thing: their southernness.

In his first letter to Lytle, Tate spoke of "interesting things . . .

16

at last stirring . . . in that part of the South which we cannot help taking about with us forever," prophesying the book that materialized three years later, *I'll Take My Stand.* Indeed, in the same week in 1927, in a letter from Tate to Ransom, the idea of a southern symposium was first mentioned.[1] Lytle's own thoughts about a southern movement began to assume concrete form in early 1929, when the Forrest biography was well along. From New York he wrote to Tate in France about devoting "the next three to five years to a lucid and forceful re-statement of our philosophy, for when the industrial powers completely dictate, there will never again be the chance."[2] Already he saw clearly his region's predicament—the traditional South poised at the brink of the modern industrial cataract—and already he had a philosophy with which to meet this predicament. His work on Forrest plus two years away from the South, first in New Haven and then in New York, had crystallized Lytle's southern identity, and now he observed the Northeast, the vanguard of the prevailing American way, from a special, increasingly articulated perspective. His philosophy had no label yet, but it would become Agrarianism.

To Tate's musings about writing a history of the South, Lytle responded enthusiastically: "Really, the idea of the history of the South is beyond words. And just at this time, before the final concentration of the empire, it will be a crying protest against that short-sighted greed which killed the goose that laid the egg. Were I ever to doubt that Biblical axiom about the sins of the fathers, New England's condition today would force a whole-hearted acceptance."[3] That is, in consequence of having led the charge for the industrial regime in the previous century, New England now endured, felt Lytle, a moral, social, and economic dehumanization. Moreover, American industrial imperialism was

1. Tate to Lytle, March 15, 1927, in Lytle Papers. See mention of a symposium in Tate's letter to Davidson, March 17, 1927, in John Tyree Fain and Thomas Daniel Young (eds.), *The Literary Correspondence of Donald Davidson and Allen Tate* (Athens, Ga., 1974), 195.

2. Lytle to Tate, January 31, 1929, in Allen Tate Papers, Box 28, Princeton University Library.

3. *Ibid.*

now about to absorb all heretofore unassimilated regions—most notably, Uncle Sam's Other Province, the South. Tate's projected history (which was never actually written) would present the Old South as an admirably ordered agrarian civilization, an alternative to the industrial society that won the Civil War and was the progenitor of modern disorder. On a smaller scale, Lytle himself was portraying just such an image of the South in the programmatic parts of his Forrest biography.

Lytle was looking at southern history not as a matter of mere antiquarian interest but as a case with contemporary relevance. As he wrote to Tate, "The hardest thing we've had to bear is that, after the murder of the South, we've had to submit to our enemies in the presentation of our case to the world. That half-baked, unseasoned victual has . . . disturbed the digestion of history." [4] To thwart heedless acquiescence in "the final concentration of the empire," Lytle felt that the shapers of southern opinion must be shown the inadequacy of the northern version of southern history ("that half-baked, unseasoned victual"). This would be a first step in bringing a restored sense of inherited ideals to the modern South.

It is no surprise, then, that Lytle was more than ready to join forces with his Vanderbilt friends and others of like mind when his former professor Donald Davidson wrote, in June, 1929, to enlist him in the project that became *I'll Take My Stand.* "Your stay here was all too short. I had much more to talk about—for instance, that Southern symposium. Did I tell you about it? If I didn't, I should like to, for you might be interested in becoming a contributor. The prospective contributors now are J.C.R. [Ransom], Tate, Stark Young, John D. Wade, and I; the general theme of the book is: Hold the fort against 'progress.'" [5] If industrialization, urbanization, and the values therein represented were "progress," then Davidson and friends did not want it. As for Lytle, holding the fort against progress was a theme already close to his heart, and further, he was back *in* the fort now, for he had gone back south to the family steadings in Tennessee

4. *Ibid.*
5. Davidson to Lytle, June 11, 1929, in Lytle Papers.

and north Alabama in May, 1929. He was never to leave again except for one brief sortie onto the New York stage in the summer of 1931 and two spring semesters teaching at the University of Iowa in 1947 and 1948.

One month after receiving Davidson's letter, Lytle received a detailed letter from Tate in France: "I understand that the Fugitives are planning a Southern offensive. In reply to Red's [Robert Penn Warren's] letter, I outlined a program of action which in my opinion, is indispensable to success. It is the formation of a society, something like the Action Francaise group. . . . Such a society should announce a whole religious, philosophical, literary, and social program, anti-industrial on the negative side, and all that implies, and, on the positive, authoritarian, agrarian, classical, aristocratic." Without such an academy subscribing to some sort of "philosophical constitution," Tate continued, the movement would fail for lack of focus. Further, he emphasized that as a group they could "create powerful opposition in the South which would clarify the issues, and create an *independent internal problem to be solved.*" Tate concluded: "I'd like your opinion. There's no use taking half measures. We must go the whole hog, or we shall end by merely brooding over the past. Instead, we must *use* the past for daring and *positive* ends."[6]

Considering how well Tate's plan of action jibed with Lytle's earlier thoughts about devoting three to five years "to a lucid and forceful re-statement of our philosophy," it is no surprise that Lytle responded enthusiastically and even considered buying a country newspaper as an organ for the movement. Tate mailed the same suggestions to Davidson ten days later, and by both Davidson's and Lytle's testimony, the proposed program had a sharp effect, giving structure and momentum to the nascent movement. As Davidson replied to Tate: "It's a tremendous stimulus just to have your letter with its grand outline of activities, and though I've been a long time in answering, I want you to know that your letter shook me up from top to toe and filled me with a new fire. Ransom and I talked it over at great length, and Andrew

6. Tate to Lytle, July 31, 1929, in Lytle Papers.

Lytle was with us, too. . . . You put us all in a stound, but not the kind of stound that lays people flat. Rather we were raised up." They were "raised up" indeed; Warren wrote Tate that "the Nashville brothers . . . are on fire with crusading zeal and the determination to lynch carpetbaggers. Andrew was at Guthrie and you can imagine the ferocity with which he expresses his approbation." The Nashville brothers were waiting only for Tate's imminent return to the United States before beginning *I'll Take My Stand* in earnest.[7]

"Hurry on home," Lytle wrote to Tate in November, 1929, inviting the Tates to come stay with him. "We should all be in this part of the South," he advised, "until the Old South movement gets organized." Eager to show the people "for what a mess of pottage they are selling their birthright," Lytle reported that he, Davidson, and Ransom were "heartily in favor" of Tate's plan. "We have had one discussion," Lytle continued, "and I am going to take them to Monteagle soon to go into it more thoroughly, but we are holding up any decisive action until you and Caroline get back."[8] (The Tates would not disembark in New York till January, 1930.)

In the meantime, a "series of earnest conferences" ensued between Lytle, Davidson, and Ransom. "Don, Andrew, and I have been doing recently a great deal of confabbing," Ransom wrote to Tate. "By the way, Andrew has more drive and courage (of the practical kind) than any of us." The three even began to hash out "a sort of Credo or Manifesto," Davidson reported, "which will serve to acquaint contributors with our aims and to furnish a definite line for articles to follow." In final form this manifesto became the "Statement of Principles," penned largely by Ransom, introducing *I'll Take My Stand*. With the new year, the southern

7. See Tate to Davidson, November 9 and August 10, 1929, Davidson to Tate, October 26, 1929, all in Fain and Young (eds.), *Literary Correspondence,* 240, 229–33, 237; Robert Penn Warren to Tate, Fall, 1929, quoted in Virginia J. Rock, "The Making and Meaning of *I'll Take My Stand*: A Study in Utopian-Conservatism, 1925–1939" (Ph.D. dissertation, University of Minnesota, 1961), 230*n.*
8. Lytle to Tate, November 26, 1929, in Tate Papers.

offensive went into full swing. By early 1930, Davidson was asking Lytle to come to staff meetings once a week, and Ransom was seeing him as the natural candidate for showing how "the actual countryman's life ought to be made livable again." Ransom wrote to Tate, "Andrew knows all about that, and it is just possible that is his true article; he sees that the farmer now lives out of a paper sack, and that farms are getting industrialized just like factories, etc., etc." By midsummer Lytle had completed "The Hind Tit" for the symposium, and by fall the symposium was published.[9]

An interesting bit of infighting having to do with the symposium's title intervened before publication. "I got a letter from Red Saturday," Tate reported to Lytle in June. "He says that the title 'I'll take my stand' is a goddamned outrage. . . . Amen." And so at Warren's impetus (he was then in England), Tate and Lytle took up the issue in Tennessee. Because it was a title with greater polemical value, the three preferred *Tracts Against Communism,* and Tate and Lytle urged this title on Davidson in a meeting in early summer. The meeting produced an understanding that Davidson would communicate Lytle's and Tate's feelings to Ransom, and then, as Lytle later reconstructed it, "if Ransom had no violent objections, we would change the title." But Davidson, who always preferred the title that eventually prevailed, did not altogether follow through on this understanding. "Don wrote him [Ransom]," stated Lytle, "but left no impression with him that the title would be changed unless he particularly disliked it. He merely told him that *Tracts Against Communism* had been suggested along with the many others, to which he [Ransom] replied that he preferred the *I'll Take My Stand.* That is, Don left the impression that it was just another title." [10]

9. Davidson to Tate, December 29, 1929, in Fain and Young (eds.), *Literary Correspondence,* 246; Ransom to Tate, January 5, 1930, quoted in Rock, "The Making and Meaning of *I'll Take My Stand,*" 236; Davidson to Tate, December 29, 1929, in Fain and Young (eds.), *Literary Correspondence,* 247; Davidson to Lytle, February 3, 1930, in Lytle Papers; Ransom to Tate, February 15, 1930, quoted in Rock, "The Making and Meaning of *I'll Take My Stand,*" 241–42.

10. Tate to Lytle, June 9, 1930, in Lytle Papers; Lytle to Tate, dated "spring 1930" many years later by Tate but almost certainly written shortly after Septem-

It was not just another title, however, as far as Lytle was concerned. He disliked the traces of defensiveness and nostalgia in the phrase from "Dixie" and preferred *Tracts Against Communism* because of its "tactical import," "selling value," and "the added surprise which the contents would give the reader." [11] In the end, though—despite more last-minute haggling about changing the title—*I'll Take My Stand: The South and the Agrarian Tradition* was the title of the book published on November 12, 1930.

The Agrarian venture gave focus and release to many of Lytle's inchoate feelings about himself and the South. Almost his first work ever to see print, "The Hind Tit" revealed a high pitch of intellectual excitement and remains crucial to understanding the evolution of his thought. Lytle has written more sophisticated essays, but this one is a cornerstone of his career. Section-by-section analysis helps to underscore the ways in which "The Hind Tit" represents the rhetoric, not of an economist, but of an artist—an important distinction.

The title of the essay shows Lytle turning naturally to metaphor and symbol, the tools of the artist. The point of the title's barnyard metaphor is that the southern farmer, Lytle's subject, has been pushed back to the "hind tit" of the national economy: "He has been turned into the runt pig in the sow's litter. Squeezed and tricked out of the best places at the side, he is forced to take the little hind tit for nourishment; and here, struggling between the sow's back legs, he has to work with every bit of his strength to keep it from being a dry hind one, and all because the suck of the others is so unreservedly gluttonous." [12] With its touch of homespun wit and aggressiveness, the title sets the morally in-

---

ber 5, 1930 (it refers at some points to a joint letter from Davidson and Ransom written on September 5), in Tate Papers.

11. Lytle to Tate, dated June, 1930, by Tate but probably written in late July, in Tate Papers.

12. Andrew Lytle, "The Hind Tit," in *I'll Take My Stand: The South and the Agrarian Tradition* (1930; rpr. Baton Rouge, 1977), 245, hereinafter cited parenthetically by page number in the text.

dignant tone for the first and third sections of the three-part essay—the tone not of a disinterested typewriter agrarian but of a fiercely loyal southern farmer.

In structure the essay consists of a long description sandwiched between two sections of argument, the first flinging down the gauntlet to the "tumble-bellied prophets" of Progress and sketching the history behind the farming South's present crisis. The middle section of the essay drops the bellicose polemics simply to render an idealized portrait of the small-farm agrarian's culture. The final section, a sort of scarifying Rake's Progress, charts the ruin of the old culture when the farmer begins to "keep books." The ledger becomes the central symbol of the essay, summing up the cash-hungry aggressiveness and abstract spirit of uncurbed industrial capitalism: "The agrarian South is bound to go when the first page is turned and the first mark crosses the ledger" (234). Thus Lytle pounds home his thesis: namely, that the South "should dread industrialism like a pizen snake" (234).

The essay proper, which is explicit about important themes implicit in Lytle's later work, begins with the statement that the American experiment has gone awry. As a nation we are allegedly wealthy, but as individuals we find this wealth a dubious boon, for "as its benefits elude us, the labors and pains of its acquisition multiply" (201). The southern farmer finds this bitter to ponder because of his historical defiance to the source of the trouble: the ascendance of an urban-industrial economy, something feared and foreseen by both Thomas Jefferson and John Calhoun. "Since 1865, an agrarian Union has been changed into an industrial empire bent on conquest of the earth's goods and ports to sell them in" (202). This industrial imperialism has produced a crisis internal to the commonwealth, or as Lytle uncompromisingly puts it, "a war to the death between technology and the ordinary human functions of living" (202). How can we save ourselves? Rejecting communism as merely a further extension of industrial debasement of the individual, Lytle prescribes "a return to a society where agriculture is practiced by most of the people" (203).

Given the present political supremacy of the industrial wealth-warrior, however, the man on the land must concern himself for now with private strategy in defending his way of life against the incursions of industrialism and its power machines. The call to become "progressive," with its promise of wealth, is a siren song that, in effect, would doom the farmer's traditional culture. "A farm is not a place to grow wealthy," Lytle asserts in one of several potent aphorisms; "it is a place to grow corn" (205). Industrializing the farm would mean capitulating to the laws of an essentially inimical economy with its "bric-a-brac culture of progress" (205).

The farmer "must close his ears to these heresies that accumulate about his head, for they roll from the tongues of false prophets" (206). Then, in the deliberately intemperate mode that is one of the delights of the essay, Lytle extends the idea of false prophecy.

> He [the southern farmer] should know that prophets do not come from cities, promising riches and store clothes. They have always come from the wilderness, stinking of goats and running with lice and telling of a different sort of treasure, one a corporation head would not understand. Until such a one comes, it is best for him to keep to his ancient ways and leave the homilies of the tumble-bellied prophets to the city man who understands such things, for on the day when he attempts to follow the whitewash metaphysics of Progress, he will be worse off than the craftsman got to be when he threw his tools away. If that day ever comes, and there are strong indications that it may, the world will see a new Lazarus, but one so miserable that no dog will lend sympathy enough to lick the fly dung from his sores. Lazarus at least groveled at the foot of the rich man's table, but the new Lazarus will not have this distinction. One cannot sit at the board of an insurance company, nor hear the workings of its gargantuan appetite whetting itself on its own digestive processes. (206)

By such images—the new Lazarus suffering in a world of faceless corporate voracity, the southern farmer sucking at the hind tit of the American sow—Lytle enriches his essay with an imaginative dimension that goes beyond discursive argument.

Next, outlining the South's economic history, Lytle emphasizes that even for the antebellum planter, implicated to some degree in a capitalist economy, wealth was not abstract stocks and bonds but real acres and slaves. The yeoman farmer had even less to do with a capitalist economy, for he was Jefferson's self-sufficient freeholder. In disposition he was such a man as a certain mere squatter who, when introduced to President Van Buren, said with composure, "Mr. Buren, the next time you come down here I want you to come out my way and ra'r around some with us boys" (213). This man, Lytle explains, "possessed nature as little as possible," yet he "enjoyed it a great deal, so well that he felt the President might be satisfied with what hospitality he had to offer" (213). Only a sound society could have so contented a man at its base.

History has too often ignored or misunderstood the antebellum yeomanry, however, and Lytle cites the journals of the New York landscape architect and travel writer Frederick Law Olmsted as an example of misconceptions about this class. Traveling the southern hill country in the 1850s, Olmsted discovered in amazement that some of the farmers thought that New York was south of Tennessee. Lytle makes this incident the basis for another of his homilies: "It was the tragedy of these people that they ever learned where New York lay, for such knowledge has taken them from a place where they knew little geography but knew it well, to places where they see much and know nothing" (211). Such audacious overstatements, Lytle trusted, would shock his audience into real thought.

Olmsted also noted the natives' enthusiasm for abandoning their plows in order to amble over and chat. "His time-ordered attitude," Lytle emphasizes, "was shocked at their lazy indifference to their work" (211). In Lytle's view, though, it was not laziness that brought the plowmen over to talk to the "quair strangy"—a view that launches an important distinction.

> This will be the most difficult task industrialism has undertaken, and on this rock its effort to industrialize the farm will probably split—to convince the farmer that it is time, not space, which has value. It will be difficult because the farmer knows that he cannot

25

control time, whereas he can wrestle with space, or at least with that particular part which is his orbit. He can stop, set, chaw, and talk, for, unable to subdue nature, it is no great matter whether he gets a little more or a little less that year from her limitless store. (211–12)

Continuing his sketch of the South's agrarian past, Lytle states that with Confederate defeat came the taint of a money economy grafted onto old agrarian ways. The plain man, becoming involved in the furnishing system, began to specialize in the money crop, usually cotton, and to rely on the merchant for feed for his stock and food for himself. Suddenly answerable to the unstable laws of a money economy, he suffered severely when cotton prices dropped. Forced into overproduction and the mortgaging of the next year's crop, he found that "something he could not understand was beginning to control his life" (214). And under such conditions white tenantry often developed, to the abasement of the no longer independent yeoman. Nonetheless, despite the damage caused by this legacy of a dual existence under antithetical economies, the early twentieth-century farmer leads a life "still largely ordered after his agrarian inheritance" (216). He stands at a fateful crossroads, though. Should he become a progressive farmer and industrialize his operations, he will begin to "think first of a money economy, last of a farmer's life," which will mean "the end of farming as a way of life" (216).

Lytle then delineates this way of life in his long, loving description of a representative farmer, *circa* 1914. In the antebellum farmhouse built by the sturdy yeoman ancestor, the farmer rises before dawn, builds the fires, and—as is the tradition—rings the bell to rouse his family. The boys feed the stock, and the womenfolk attend to the ritual of milking, straining, cooling, and churning—a long but valuable process, "because insomuch as it has taken time and care and intelligence, by that much does it have a meaning" (223). Further, Lytle emphasizes the "mighty variety" that fills the day of each family member, for in it lies an implicit rebuke to the drudgery and meaninglessness of work in a mechanized setting (223).

The midday meal, unhurried and full of conversation, is a social event with "a great deal of form" (225). On the table is the "abundance of nature" with "its bulging-breasted fowls, deep-yellow butter and creamy milk, fat beans and juicy corn, and its potatoes flavored like pecans" (227). This arcadian farmer has "the satisfaction of well-being, because he has not yet come to look upon his produce at so many cents a pound" (227). Additionally, the food has special meaning because everyone at the table "has had something to do with the long and intricate procession from the ground to the table" (227). Unlike the city dweller, for whom rain is little more than the spoiler of a picnic, the farmer is on entirely different terms with nature. "The fullness of meaning that rain and the elements extend to the farmer is all contained in a mess of beans, a plate of potatoes, or a dish of sallet" (227). As for the farmer's superstitions—checking to see if the moon is holding water, burning the hearth fire through May as a charm for good crops—such practices are part of his reverent struggle with a world he recognizes to be beyond the scientist's manipulations.

Finally, when day is done or crops are laid by, there are activities that sum up the culture and bind the community: play-parties, square dances, Sacred Harp gatherings, political barbecues. The continuity of this neighborhood culture is such that even the old grandmother is still a part of the festivities, not alienated by time as she would be in the swiftly-changing world of urban industrialism:

> Even mammy, if the rheumaticks had not frozen her jints, would put on her hickory-staved bonnet, a fresh-starched apron, and mount the waggin with the rest and drive to the singing and lift her cracked voice as the leader "h'isted" the tune, or at the barbecue pat her feet in time with the whining fiddle and think of better days when she and her old man balanced to "Cairo ladies, show yore-self," or "Jenny, the Flower of Kildare," until the sweat poured from her strong back, gluing the gray linen dress to her shoulders and ballooning it in places with air caught in the swing. (233–34)

With rich details and dialect words, such passages make clear that Lytle invests as much emotion in this anatomy of a way of life—almost entirely through character and image—as in the two fiercer sections of more conventional argument. Pastoral description of such a life constitutes a covert argument that speaks to the harried urbanite every bit as much as to the embattled farmer. For it was hoped that agriculture, an ideal form of labor, might become "the model to which the other forms approach as well as they may."[13]

The middle section states, in effect, what it means to be a southern farmer. Already possessing such a stable and fulfilling life, why should he adopt the restless state of mind of industrialism? What could "progress" do for him? The last section of the essay answers this question as it traces the decline of the "typical" farmer when he begins to "keep books," that is, when he begins to give first place to the ever-escalating demands of a money economy.

First, says Lytle, with progressivism comes the highway, which imperils the South's culture-sustaining provincialism. (Thoreau had said in his attack on materialism, "We do not ride on the railroad; it rides upon us.") The asphalt roads mean bad footing for the farmer's mules, higher property taxes, and the influx of high-pressure salesmen. The farmer sells his mules and buys a tractor, but this displaces his sons from much of their former work. Thus begins the "home-breaking," for "time is money now, not property, and the boys can't hang around the place draining it of its substance" (236). The farmer buys a truck, then a car, and soon feels the weight of gasoline bills, bank loans, and installment payments. He gradually begins to have too little time for raising a garden and killing his own meat; with newfangled plows and artificial fertilizers he concentrates on the money crop, his one-time self-sufficiency now a lost dream. With each step he damages his old way of life, which traditionally preferred "religion to science, handcrafts to technology, the inertia of the fields to the acceleration of industry, and leisure to nervous prostration" (234).

The farmer becomes the victim of a great deception, for he finds that nature is far from reducible to man's utter control.

13. "Statement of Principles," in *I'll Take My Stand*, xlvii.

"When he bought the various machines which roll where the mules stood and shivered the flies from their backs, he was told that he might regulate, or get ahead of, nature. He finds to his sorrow that he is still unable to control the elements. When it fails to rain and his fields are burning, he has no God to pray to to make it rain. Science can put the crops in, but it can't bring them out of the ground" (238). When the farmer tries to recover his "ancient bearings," he finds "a vast propaganda" out to "uplift" him, telling him that his ancestors were uncultured and illiterate (242). The South can "come to glory," say all the satraps of industrialism, by denying its heritage and swapping its culture "for machine-made bric-a-brac" (243). This, Lytle says incisively, is "nothing but demoniacally clever high-pressure sales talk to unload the over-producing merchandize of industrialism" (242–43).

Further, because a money economy inevitably leads the farmer to overextend himself, there is the danger of "an absentee-landlordism far worse than that which afflicted the continent at the breakdown of mediaeval society. . . . Mortgage companies, insurance companies, banks, and bonding-houses that are forced to take over the land of free men . . . what will be the social relationship? What can an abstract corporation like an insurance company, whose occupation is statistics and whose faro-bank can never lose, know of a farmer's life? What can their calculations do before droughts, floods, the boll weevil, hails, and rainy seasons?" (243). The questions reflect a belief central to Lytle's attack on the dehumanizing character of capitalism—namely, that capitalism is ultimately abstract and therefore insensitive to the concrete relationships of man to man and man to nature, relationships that teach man his limitations and his need for manners, mores, and institutions.

To protect his traditional way of life, the farmer must keep the money crop in second place and refuse the merchandise of industrialism. "Throw out the radio," advises Lytle in an epigram, "and take down the fiddle from the wall" (244). The southerner should protect his heritage, diminished though it may be. "It is our own, and if we have to spit in the water-bucket to keep it our own, we had better do it" (245). Thus ends the essay, of whose forty-five pages only one is devoted to practical recommendations and strategy for maintaining old-style farming in the South. Practical politics and economics are simply not part of the main argument of the essay, for Lytle writes as an artist, not as a social engineer.

Let the southerner protect his heritage, preserve his southernness, cherish his inherited sense of himself—in other words, recognize himself as both the shaper and creature of history. Further, let him see modernism for what it is. Let him not become a mere cipher in some spurious notion of economic and cultural determinism, Lytle says, for he has less to gain and more to lose than he may well realize. Stated thus, the import of "The Hind Tit" hardly seems to be foolish neo-Confederate romanticism, yet the essay was widely attacked as such. The contemporary misunderstandings of *I'll Take My Stand,* however, have been oft quoted and oft set to rights. As prologue to a consideration of the essential qualities of Lytle's Agrarianism, I refer to a much wiser and more recent reaction to the Agrarian symposium, though perhaps one that still misjudges the lasting appeal of *I'll Take My Stand.*

In his influential book *The Burden of Southern History,* C. Vann Woodward ponders the issue of how one defines the essence of southernness. For Woodward the agrarian formulation of *I'll Take My Stand* will not hold up as a durable definition of the southern way of life. To champion an anti-industrial, farm-rooted way of life as the sine qua non of southernness, he argues, was and is to enlist in "a second lost cause." In view of the South's pell-mell defection since 1930 to the American industrial pattern, Agrarianism ostensibly "contains no promise of continuity and endurance for the Southern tradition." Woodward recommends that the best way for the South to define itself is not by dreaming of "an ephemeral economic order" but simply by accepting the uniqueness of "the collective experience of the Southern people," their un-American legacy of defeat, hardship, guilt, and communal attachment to place. Memory of this unique heritage, suggests Woodward, can also counterbalance prevailing American legends of success, abundace, innocence, and rootless unrestraint. The South's history, in other words, can stand as a sort of fifth column against unthinking worship of that ersatz religion, the American Way of Life. It is a salutary recommendation, close to what Agrarianism is all about in a way that is too often underestimated.[14]

Woodward's judgment on *I'll Take My Stand* is certainly warranted by what he takes to be the core of Agrarianism—its advocacy of the farm over the factory. However, this is to define Agrarianism too narrowly, though the Agrarians themselves must share the blame ("Agrarian *versus* Industrial" are the terms of the "Statement of Principles"). Agrarianism, in the final analysis, was and is a reaffirmation of the deepest values of Western civilization. In its essentials, it is the still-relevant fifth column that Woodward calls for. In his consideration of the symposium's achievement, Louis Rubin states it this way: "The lasting qualities of *I'll Take My Stand* . . . have to do not with its supposed 'alternative' to an industrial society, but with its assertion of permanent, ongoing humane values, as a protest against the dehumanizing possibilities of that society."[15]

Even though Lytle's essay calls upon the specific image of the farm more than any other in the symposium, he exemplifies the contributors for whom *Agrarian* suggested more than farming and *Industrial* suggested more than manufacturing. As he later remarked, "The agrarian period was a conscious and critical attack, out of a large knowledge, upon the New South men as men traduced by the enemy. This was called Industrialism, but it was a poor name." Lytle would later use the word *Faustian* to more nearly suggest the soul selling, power worship, and irreligious exaltation of the individual will that he deplored in modernism.[16]

14. C. Vann Woodward, *The Burden of Southern History* (Rev. ed.; Baton Rouge, 1968), 21, 25.

15. Louis D. Rubin, Jr., *The Wary Fugitives: Four Poets and the South* (Baton Rouge, 1978), 245.

16. Andrew Lytle, "A Summing Up," *Shenandoah,* VI (Summer, 1955), 31. See his use of the word *Faustian* in, for instance, "Foreword to *A Novel, a Novella*

As for the word *Agrarian,* the prepublication correspondence shows how much more it meant than soil tilling. Lytle's all-embracing desire to show the populace "for what a mess of pottage they are selling their birthright" was a desire for far-ranging protest, not for mere back-to-the-plow economics. In view of this, it is understandable that Lytle later saw the term *Agrarian* as a "tactical error," a misleadingly "exclusive" word too limited to describe their protest adequately.[17]

Certainly "The Hind Tit" deals with traditional farming versus progressive farming—a specific, ostensibly practical matter. But farming provides the concrete terms of a broader argument involving philosophy and religion, not merely economics. The surface terms may be plowing with mules versus plowing with tractors, but the ultimate, detachable terms are freedom versus servility, and family-, community-, and religious-consciousness versus alienation from family, community, and God. The strategy of Lytle's essay is to arrange alternatives in extreme terms—to reveal the difference between agriculture and agribusiness, for instance, as ultimately the difference between culture and business. Exaggeration is a primary way to get through to a people dulled by the blandishments of progressive propaganda, and such was Lytle's conception of his audience.

The specifics, the contemporary socioeconomics of "The Hind Tit," are the chaff that has been winnowed away by time, and what endure are the affirmation of a humane tradition and the all-too-prophetic indictments of the commercial spirit. It is hard to accept Lytle's contention that rural electrification reduces the farmer's wife to being a "drudge," an "assistant to machines," but to reject the essay on this score is to judge it on the wrong grounds (237). Similarly, contemporary reviewers who dismissed Lytle and the other Agrarians as mere "sufferers from nostalgic vapors" were unable to see the essential nature of *I'll Take My Stand* as a castigation of the age in the tradition of James Fenimore

---

and *Four Stories,"* in *The Hero with the Private Parts* (Baton Rouge, 1966), 201, volume hereinafter cited in notes as Lytle, *Hero.*

17. Lytle to Tate, November 26, 1929, in Tate Papers; Andrew Lytle, "The Agrarians Today: A Symposium," *Shenandoah,* III (Summer, 1952), 31.

Cooper's *The American Democrat,* Henry David Thoreau's *Walden,* and Ralph Waldo Emerson's "The American Scholar." [18] Lytle was certainly no naïve archaist, no vestigial Luddite; he was too much of a realist to fantasize a literal, across-the-board rescission of the industrial era. Some of his remarks at the Fugitives' Reunion in 1956 speak to this point; to wit, he had been well aware in 1930, he remembered, that a wholesale return to a simple agrarian society, given the combative, power-state conditions of international affairs, would have been suicidal. "If you destroyed the industrial set-up, then we would be slaves." [19] However, to have admitted all such qualifications and practicalities into "The Hind Tit" would have been to vitiate the force of its social and moral arguments that rise above the din of international politics.

Lytle wrote "The Hind Tit" as an "ideal or romantic version of what the plain farmer—the yeoman farmer—was; but," he continues, "I was making the point deliberately, as a kind of a literary exercise." [20] By overstating his case in this literary exercise, he could persuasively define what "those who have chewed the mad root's poison," the agents of so-called progress, really considered "the goods and riches of the earth," which were not the goods and riches of a healthy culture (203, 207). A reverent life of aesthetic possibilities and community order was the vision of society behind Lytle's statement, "A farm is not a place to grow wealthy; it is a place to grow corn" (205). The devotees of Progress, Lytle made clear, would always be mystified by such a statement, for they ultimately reduce all endeavor to a cash nexus, which leads to exploitation of both man and nature. Thus the issue was spelled out in no uncertain language: unless twentieth-century man recognized and asserted his natural rights, he would be doomed "to hop about like sodium on water, burning up in his own energy" (202).

At the root of such warnings was plainly a desire to expose the

18. H. L. Mencken, "Uprising in the Confederacy," *American Mercury,* XXII (1931), 380. On the issue of the symposium's literary tradition, see Rubin, *The Wary Fugitives,* especially 237–40.

19. Rob Roy Purdy (ed.), *Fugitives' Reunion: Conversations at Vanderbilt, May 3–5, 1956* (Nashville, 1959), 214.

20. *Ibid.*

heresies of industrial capitalism and to assert the dignity and freedom that are man's deserving. To put such a desire into action through art had its own innate value, regardless of success or failure in the workaday world. Lytle's other, more specific desire was to encourage the survival of the small farm as a leaven in the lump of the nation. Lytle has recently reemphasized that the predominantly small-farm character of the South was, in 1930, capable of enduring into the future, though it was at a critical juncture, and conscious, practical effort could have kept it vital.[21] There is no doubt that Lytle was interested in just such effort toward practical action, utilizing Agrarianism to some degree as a social program, as prescriptive economics. Shun rural electrification, even make your own shoes, advised Lytle, and to this extent the ultimate and universal terms of his Agrarianism kept company with practicalities altogether harder to accept, though Lytle willfully exaggerated such things much in the manner of *Walden*. Perhaps the farmer can buy shoes "for half the labor he will put into their creation," but there are hidden costs, as Lytle uncompromisingly points out in Thoreauvian fashion. "If the cash price paid for shoes were the only cost, it would be bad economy to make shoes at home. Unfortunately, the matter is not so simple: the fifteen-hundred-dollar tractor, the thousand-dollar truck, the cost of transportation to and from town, all the cost of indirect taxation, every part of the money economy, enters into the price of shoes" (245).

Lytle (unlike Tate) simply did not feel the need to distance himself from hopes and concerns about practical results. As Tate wrote in a letter to Davidson:

> There is one feature of our movement that calls for comment. We are not in the least divided, but we exhibit two sorts of minds. You and Andrew seem to constitute one sort—the belief in the eventual success, in the practical sense, of the movement. The other mind is that of Ransom and Warren and myself [Tate proved to be wrong about Ransom]. I gather than Ransom agrees with me that the issue on the plane of action is uncertain. At least I am

---

21. Lytle, "They Took Their Stand," 118.

wholly sceptical on that point. . . . I believe that there is enough
value to satisfy me in the affirmation, in all its consequences, in-
cluding action, of value.[22]

Lytle did interest himself in Agrarianism as a literal, potentially
feasible mode of life, but this did not attenuate his broader belief
in Agrarianism as an attitude, a philosophy for interpreting life—
or as Tate put it, an "affirmation . . . of value" worth making for
its own sake.

Whether or not it was manifest destiny that the traditional,
small-farm South go out on the wave that industrialism came in
on, the small-farm South *is* largely gone now. However, Lytle's
essay addressing that older way of life remains as something more
than a dusty historical footnote. Attesting to its still-resonant
appeal are recent commentaries on the artistry and continuing
relevance of *I'll Take My Stand* that single out "The Hind Tit" for
special praise.[23] The longest of the symposium's twelve essays, it
is arguably the most passionate. Tate thought it in some ways the
best. As he wrote to fellow Agrarian John Gould Fletcher when
I'll Take My Stand came out: "I believe that Lytle's essay in some
ways is the most powerful; it is absolutely uncompromising, it is
perfectly concrete in its argument, and even though it may be
considered a little impracticable by the faint-hearted, it remains
always to be seen what practicability is. He directly wards off
from us any charge of Southern-backward-looking; he is looking
at the concrete, present thing as a starting point."[24] The success
of Lytle's argument lies not in its practicability or impracticability.
Its merit lies in stimulating the friendly and challenging the hos-

22. Tate to Davidson, November 9, 1929, in Fain and Young (eds.), *Literary
Correspondence,* 241.
23. See, for instance, M. Thomas Inge, "The Continuing Relevance of *I'll Take
My Stand,*" *Mississippi Quarterly,* XXXIII (1980), 445–60; Martha E. Cook,
"The Artistry of *I'll Take My Stand,*" *Mississippi Quarterly,* XXXIII (1980),
425–32; Lucinda H. MacKethan, "*I'll Take My Stand:* The Relevance of the Agrarian Vision," *Virginia Quarterly Review,* LVI (1980), 577–95; Richard Gray, *The
Literature of Memory: Modern Writers of the American South* (Baltimore,
1977), 47–51.
24. Tate to John Gould Fletcher, November 4, 1930, quoted in Rock, "The
Making and Meaning of *I'll Take My Stand,*" 300.

tile to judge life according to the standards of universal human value that Lytle defines—and to determine practicability within those same parameters.

To stress what is universal, *more* than southern, in Lytle's Agrarianism hardly means that southern experience is tangential to Agrarianism. Ignoring Lytle's experience as a southerner in the first three decades of the twentieth century makes it impossible to imagine "The Hind Tit" even being written. Indeed, the tension between the two world views of the old life and the new life "came to Tennessee after the world war with greater force than after the Civil War," Lytle has written. In Middle Tennessee at the age of twenty-seven, Lytle saw his childhood community and his region as a whole caught in the machinery of rapid change from one way of life to another. During his childhood, Lytle later stated, "Murfreesboro was a real community. . . . We all seemed to move, to meet and part, as ourselves among ourselves" in that "country society, which ours was and is no more." [25] In sum, having grown up in the premodern South (for the South came late to the power age), Lytle found modernism a shock to his inherited sense of himself, and this was the impetus for "The Hind Tit," his cry of protest. He recognized, however, that like it or not he was *of* the power age, and he refused to retreat into a jewel-weighted past, to resign himself to backward-looking nostalgia. He spoke to the power age by building images of the clash between old and new, by dramatizing modern man's predicament.

25. Andrew Lytle, "A Summing Up," 34, and *A Wake for the Living: A Family Chronicle* (New York, 1975), 13, 11, 3.

III

In the American Backwoods:
Agrarianism After *I'll Take My Stand*

Neither Lytle nor his brothers-in-arms intended to retire from the field after firing Agrarianism's first (and best) volley in *I'll Take My Stand*, and during the next eight years, Lytle devoted considerable energy to the cause in broadsides, book reviews, letters to newspapers, small-farm encomiums, and rereadings of history. Indeed, Davidson would remark to Tate in 1932 that "Andrew is about the only one of us who has had the crusading spirit."[1] Throughout this period from 1930 until his marriage in 1938, home for Lytle was Cornsilk Farm, his father's plantation near Guntersville, Alabama. He also spent time at his grandmother Nelson's in Murfreesboro; at Southwestern University in Memphis, where he spent part of 1936 teaching history; and at Benfolly, the Tates' country house near Clarksville, where he met and learned from Ford Madox Ford. Lytle helped with Cornsilk—overseeing laborers, making sorghum, working in the gar-

1. Davidson to Tate, October 29, 1932, in John Tyree Fain and Thomas Daniel Young (eds.), *The Literary Correspondence of Donald Davidson and Allen Tate* (Athens, Ga., 1974), 275.

den—but it was in these years that he discovered and settled down seriously to his true profession, the writing of fiction.

In the period immediately following publication of *I'll Take My Stand,* however, writing fiction was not of primary importance to Lytle. In the fall and winter of 1930–31, he was pressing hard toward the conclusion of *Bedford Forrest,* which he finished while staying with the Tates at Benfolly. Nevertheless, he found time to go to Ransom's November and January debates against Stringfellow Barr in Richmond and Chattanooga, at the latter of which Lytle was said to have "captured the crowd" during postdebate discussions. Just a month after publication of *I'll Take My Stand,* Lytle and Tate wrote a "Memorandum for Generals Davidson, Ransom, Lanier" about putting together a prospectus for a follow-up symposium. Lytle agreed with Tate that their job as Agrarians was "not to carry out the details of a program," but he hoped all the same for a second book that would include a consideration of practical "ways and means" in addition to its broad philosophizing.[2] Talk about this book would extend over five years, though, before Tate and Herbert Agar organized *Who Owns America?,* the nearest thing to a sequel that ever materialized.

Despite the lack of much consolidated action, however, the movement did go forward, and in addition to the publication of *Bedford Forrest,* 1931 saw the first of Lytle's many essay-reviews on the Agrarian cause. "The Lincoln Myth," appearing in the *Virginia Quarterly Review,* admired Edgar Lee Masters' *Lincoln, the Man* for debunking the northern fiction of Lincoln as the pure, Union-cherishing "Jeffersonian railsplitter"—a myth, said Lytle, that "helps to sustain the industrial imperialism which was made possible by Lincoln's successful prosecution of the war." In the same vein was a 1932 review of books on the antebellum southern nationalists Robert Barnwell Rhett and Edmund Ruffin. These old ghosts, wrote Lytle, have made a timely appearance to haunt the air of a nation on the brink of total economic and so-

2. Davidson to Tate, January 14, 1931, in *ibid.,* 259; Lytle and Tate to Davidson, Ransom, and Lyle Lanier, December 11, 1930, in Lytle Papers; Lytle to Tate, February 23, 1933, in Tate Papers.

cial ruin, for "there is an uninterrupted congruity between the events which these two radicals helped to define and the present economic distress." These lives of Rhett and Ruffin, Lytle concluded, should "offer a program: the revival of some form of agrarianism." Again, in a review of a Sherman biography in 1933, Lytle plumped for Agrarianism by denouncing the book as "a glorification of Sherman, Grant, and the Northern chieftains not as individuals but as heroes of the centralizing, industrial element which destroyed the early American idea of the Union and has now brought the country, after seventy years of loot, to the brink of anarchy and revolution." Marking the end of this book-review campaign was a long essay in 1938 on Calhoun (whose biography Lytle had considered writing in the early 1930s), for by this date Lytle's fiery tone had given way to a more elegiac and more strictly historical pondering of the past.[3]

The most significant of Lytle's Agrarian efforts in these years were two long essays in the *American Review*—"The Backwoods Progression" and "John Taylor and the Political Economy of Agriculture"—and also his essay "The Small Farm Secures the State" in *Who Owns America?* The first of these essays, especially, was of great importance in the evolution of Lytle's conception of Agrarianism and the South.

Published in September, 1933, "The Backwoods Progression" centers on the American backwoods—the South—as a reflection of an "agrarian state of mind" in opposition to the "middle class state of mind" of the rest of the nation. In this essay Lytle broadens the nature of his southern allegiance by picturing the antebellum South as a New World reflection of an older Christian inheritance.[4] A radically conservative, Spengler-influenced read-

3. Andrew Lytle, "The Lincoln Myth," *Virginia Quarterly Review,* VII (1931), 621, 624; "Principles of Secession," *Hound and Horn,* V (1932), 688, 693—review of Laura White, *Robert Barnwell Rhett, Father of Secession,* and Avery Craven, *Edmund Ruffin, Southerner;* "A Tactical Blunder," *Virginia Quarterly Review,* IX (1933), 301—review of Lloyd Lewis, *Sherman: Fighting Prophet;* and "John C. Calhoun," *Southern Review,* 1st ser., III (1938), 510–30—review of Arthur Styron, *The Cast Iron Man: John C. Calhoun and American Democracy.*

4. Andrew Lytle, "The Backwoods Progression," *American Review,* I (1933), 417, hereinafter cited parenthetically by page number in the text. This essay was

ing of English and American history, the essay connects the agrarian mentality to ostensible roots in feudalism and sketches its course—the backwoods progression—through history into the present.

Whereas the southern farmer at the hind tit of the national sow had been the dominant image behind Lytle's first essay, this second major essay focuses on the image of the backwoods pioneer, a mythic figure, as Lytle sees him, who "will probably epitomize North American civilization for world history as the crusader epitomizes Christian Feudalism" (409). The legacy of the backwoodsman, Lytle says, is the one feature held in common by the different regions of this "no longer commonly-minded country," and on those infrequent occasions when the modern citizen ponders his origin, it is the backwoodsman alone who seems to bear meaning for him. Unfortunately, the back-woodsman's strength and daring have been "abstracted into a state of mind which gives directly to the big business man his ruthless drive, to the gangster a cruel realism, and to the walkers of asphalt a vicarious feeling of power which readily makes them tools of those who possess power" (409). It is high time, then, declares Lytle, to clarify the image of the backwoodsman.

The original backwoodsmen, though hardy enough, were not aggressive, exploitative, power-craving men. In fact, the earliest backwoodsmen, such as the lubberlanders in North Carolina, had tried to get away from the exploiters, that is, the New World's Tory gentry and their dreams of empire. When the Virginia grandee William Byrd spoke contemptuously of the

---

first offered as a contribution to W. W. Couch's *Culture in the South,* but Couch seems to have been captious about the essay's freewheeling, thoroughly un-statistical nature. As Lytle reported to Davidson in a dialect letter, "That North Carolina feller. We can't git together. The only reason I decided to contribute was in the hopes that I could strike a blow in the enemy camp, and since I can't do that, I don't want to git thar stink on me. . . . The fool wanted to know what kind of winder curtains folks living five miles from the highway hung in their win-dows. Anybody that ain't got no more judgment than to think people living five miles from the highways are backwoodsmen won't do to argy with." Lytle to Davidson, November 2, 1932, in Davidson Papers.

backwoodsmen's "thorough Aversion to Labor" and "Disposition to Laziness," he said more about himself than about them, for laziness could not explain their filing off to North Carolina nearly so well as could their fear of oppression in colonial Virginia.[5]

Seeing the colonial exploiter-gentleman as the agent of disruptive forces dating back to the crumbling of feudalism, Lytle delineates the backwoodsman's context within Western, not just American, history. In sixteenth-century England, says Lytle, the feudal concept of kingship began to be secularized, and the Church began to lose its influence and integrity. The eventual consequence of the medieval polity's collapse—to summarize Lytle's argument—was a secular state founded on money and property, the spiritual significance of miter and scepter a dead letter. "By the time of the Whig revolution of 1688," Lytle alleges, "the idea of the State had completely changed in the English world" to the belief that "the State exists for private property . . . for the private will" (412, 413). This overreaching exaltation of the private will, variously called "Faustian," "Promethean," and "Puritan," is the great sin recurrently mentioned in Lytle's essays and depicted in his fiction.

Thus came about "the moral revolution that changed the mediaeval concept of the economic commodity from the thing-to-be-used to the thing-to-be-sold: the revolution at the bottom of the anarchy of the modern world" (413). Powering this revolution was the aggressive, "will-full" man who impiously viewed the world as "a possession answerable to the commands of his desire" (413). Discovery of the New World promised not only a haven for the downtrodden, displaced, and disaffected but also a new ground for exploitation by "men already masters of the technique of conquest" (413). The New World backwoodsman, then, was fleeing "from the same sort of domestic conqueror he had encountered in the old world" (413).

Shifting his attention to the American Revolution, Lytle points

5. William Byrd, *Histories of the Dividing Line Betwixt Virginia and North Carolina* (Gloucester, Mass., 1984), 92.

out that the colonies themselves were England's backwoods, possessing a self-dependent spirit on account of which "the exploiting gentry in the old world and their Tory allies in the new lost a continent" (414). However, when parties formed in the new nation, they were familiar enemies in new guises—the agrarian and backwoods Republican and the middle-class and exploitative Federalist. The Republican Jefferson, Lytle continues, "hoped to produce a stable farming society, predominantly yeoman, in which the head of every family might be assured of an independent living for his dependents and the promise of security for his posterity," and "for one precious moment" he had a chance to institute just such an agrarian state and to ground it on "the dogma of one religion" (415). But with his legislation for abandoning primogeniture and separating church and state, Jefferson showed himself confused in philosophy, and like the Federalists, he accepted the idea of a secular state meant to guarantee—as Lytle would have it—profane possession.

From the philosophically confused struggle between Republicans and Federalists emerged the issue that set the stage for the sixty-year struggle that would culminate in the Civil War: which would prevail, the middle-class, capitalist East or the agrarian, planter-led South? (The West, still in transition, had as yet no clear allegiance, but as a farming section its proper alliance was with the South [418].) Fueled and shaped by cotton, slavery, and the plantocracy, the South developed a feudalism "greatly different from European feudalism, but preserving the inertia and fixing the form so that the European tradition could be preserved" (422). With an alien race as servant class, the planter had no oppressive designs on the small farmer, continues Lytle; their common anticapitalistic interests united them, and the talented plain man often moved up into the ranks of the plantocracy. Therefore, with planter as feudal lord and Jeffersonian farmer as yeoman, this evolution toward a feudalistic "social and spiritual unity" signified a southern agrarian nation in resistance to a Union founded on capitalistic private property. With Confederate defeat, however, went "the last great check to the imperialism of

Big Business," and the capitalist element could make its long-delayed conquest of the continent (425).

So, in twentieth-century America the trees of the backwoods are gone, but, maintains Lytle, "it is not trees which define the backwoods" (427). The depression hobo is the long hunter's spiritual heir, symbolizing all outcasts of capitalism—those supplanted by machines, those uprooted by a money economy, and those harboring some perception of a separate destiny. Who speaks for them? The South, Lytle asserts, remains the historical seat of opposition and thus the spiritual backwoods of the nation. (At this point the essay gains its greatest intensity.) Capitalism may finally have annexed the South, but there is still the attachment of its inhabitants to ancestral ways. "It has become the fashion to forget this," writes Lytle, "but fashions change; tradition lodges in the blood" (430). Then, in apocalyptic conclusion, Lytle declares that the South "represents the only group of states in this country with enough form left to shake off their lethargy when the walls of steel and concrete tumble down upon our heads; when the electric webs break loose from their poles to dart and sting like scorpions" (434).

The liberal quip that conservatism is the art of keeping up with yesterday would scarcely offend Lytle, and for him that ideal yesterday, as "The Backwoods Progression" shows, occurred long ago. Lytle in this essay places his passionate attachment to the South within the context of the sweep of Western history. In doing so, he links his southern loyalties to the image of wholeness and order he descries in the High Middle Ages—an image summed up in the word *Christendom.* The rise of the bourgeoisie, Henry VIII's sacking of the monasteries, the Stuart perversion of rule by divine right, the Whig revolt of 1688, and particularly the defeat of the Confederacy—Anglo history since the Middle Ages, according to Lytle's world view, has seen Faustian secularism and materialism go from success to success. This context explains Lytle's later-stated view of Agrarianism as a reexamination of "a set of principles and ideas whose history was as old as Christendom." In resistance to the confusion of modern values, Lytle to some degree willed himself into a conservative intellectual framework much in the same way that T. S. Eliot declared himself "classicist in literature, royalist in politics and anglo-catholic in religion."[6] But it was not entirely an intellectual matter. Lytle's traditionalism—his looking backward to an abused inheritance as opposed to the typical modern's gaze forward into the secular millenium—had its moorings in a gene-deep, sometimes appalled fascination with what was different about his region.

In "The Backwoods Progression," the effect of Oswald Spengler's *The Decline of the West* shows itself in Lytle's terminology and in his broad sense of modern civilization's disintegration. As Lytle told Tate, who had offered some suggestions on the essay's rough draft, "I was reading the second volume of Spengler at the time, and he influenced me considerably." That the author of "The Hind Tit" found much in Spengler to adapt to his own uses is no surprise, as a few representative passages from Volume II of *The Decline of the West* can amply explain. Spengler writes, for instance, that "the economic foundation of the great Culture is always a mankind that adheres fast to the soil," and he describes the rise of the megalopolis also in terms an Agrarian could appreciate: "Long, long ago the country bore the country-town and nourished it with her best blood. Now the giant city sucks the country dry, insatiably and incessantly demanding and devouring fresh streams of men, till it wearies and dies in the midst of an almost uninhabited waste of country."

The city, according to Spengler's comparative interpretation of the main cultures in history, invariably "assumes the lead and control of economic history in replacing the primitive values of the land, which are forever inseparable from the life and thought of the rustic, by the *absolute idea of money* as distinct from goods." Thus, when Culture hardens into that increasingly sterile entity that Spengler calls Civilization, money becomes "a form of

6. Lytle, "The Agrarians Today," 30; T. S. Eliot, *For Lancelot Andrewes* (London, 1928), ix.

the activity of [man's] waking-consciousness, having no longer any roots in Being. This is the basis of its monstrous power over every beginning Civilization, which is always an unconditional dictatorship of money."[7]

Rejecting concepts of linear progress, Spengler sees history as organism: a culture develops like the life cycle of an organism, from birth to decay, or—to use his most frequent metaphor— from the agricultural, feudal spring of the High Middle Ages in Western culture to the capitalistic, plutocratic winter just now beginning. Spengler's "decline of the West" might be said to be the rise of the middle class, begun with the Reformation; for the acquisitive middle class's main purpose, according to Spengler, is the destruction of the two soil-rooted prime estates, the nobility and the priesthood. "The urban [middle-class] intellect reforms the great religion of the springtime and sets up by the side of the old religion of noble and priest, the new religion of the Tiers État, *liberal science.*"[8] Finally, with modern civilization the middle class fulfills its destructive destiny by erecting cities in which the rootless, money-bewitched intellect thrives, its greatest feats consisting merely of applying science to industry.

Reading Spengler, Lytle found a massive theoretical framework supporting most of his southern instincts—the instincts he had followed in attacking so-called progressivism in "The Hind Tit." Building on Spengler, "The Backwoods Progression" extended Lytle's Agrarianism beyond what "The Hind Tit" had said about the cancer of progressivism in the postbellum south to show that the disease was not endemic but epidemic, and had been for a long time. Standing in the afterwash of the centuries, Lytle came away from reading Spengler with an even sharper perception of Western cultural decay and with a superstructure of history in which to place his feelings about the South. Lytle did not wholly accept what was deterministic in Spengler's philosophy, but his

7. Lytle to Tate, May 21, 1933, in Tate Papers; Oswald Spengler, *The Decline of the West: Perspectives of World-History,* trans. Charles Francis Atkinson (New York, 1928), 474*n,* 102, 97, 98.
8. Spengler, *The Decline of the West,* 97.

premonition of a coming "Caesarian condition of servility" was entirely Spenglerian, as was his general view of the ruinous effect of middle-class materialism and impiety on the course of Western history (434). Lytle's anatomy of Old South society was certainly his own, Spengler having said almost nothing about the American South, but he used Spengler in the course of interpreting that society as a reflection of the old medieval polity—a reflection sufficient, thought Lytle, to fix the form "so that the European tradition could be preserved' (422). The modern South bears few traces of the antebellum, anticapitalist order, but "tradition lodges in the blood" and memories endure. In however sullen and degraded a form, there remains, asserted Lytle, a southern consciousness of higher goods than capitalism can offer. The South has not been emasculated spiritually and thus still represents an agrarian state of mind opposed to the "middle-class moneyed princes" and all they stand for (433).

Lytle's historicity in all of this is matter for controversy, but in terms of Lytle the literary man, it does not matter whether his historical theorizing cleaves to documentable fact or is creative misinterpretation.[9] What I wish to document is the tenor of his thought and the way it becomes translated into art. And—to extrapolate from "The Hind Tit" and "The Backwoods Progression"—the tenor of his thought is radically conservative in its view of man, God, and the state, and deeply traditionalist in its distress over the disappearance of community and the widespread anomie that results. For Lytle, man is decidedly *not* self-defining, perfectible, or the measure of all things. Instead, human nature is stained with the deep dye of original sin. Attempts to go beyond human limitations are shot through with destructive hubris and typically end in catastrophe. This view is essentially Augustinian in its awareness of evil and in its apprehension, as

9. One might mention, though, that the Marxist historian Eugene Genovese (ergo presumably dispassionate in these matters) has in three well-documented books said that southern planter society, "in its spirit and fundamental direction, represented the antithesis of capitalism, however many compromises it had to make [with capitalism]." Quotation from *The Political Economy of Slavery* (New York, 1967), 23.

Lytle once described it, of "the City of God as the end of the drama."[10]

Religion is dealt with only glancingly in "The Backwoods Progression." Nevertheless, the essay reveals one of Lytle's root assumptions about the power and proper role of religion, namely, that the religious sensibility determines the economic structure and not the other way around. The High Middle Ages constitute an ideal in Lytle's mind largely for this very reason. The power of the king, the craft of the artisan, indeed, all the elements and duties of this society, were felt to rest in the Godhead of medieval Christian belief; that is, the Christian moral and spiritual center of medieval life shaped the form and values of its feudalism. Partly out of such musings, Lytle came to look on Agrarianism as a defense of what was left of a Christendom that was perhaps mythical but no less powerful as an image. So, in one sense, Agrarianism became for Lytle a holy war against infidels, all those in conscious or unconscious violation of fealty to the divine. Entirely transmuted into art, this religious dimension in Lytle's Agrarianism has its most striking fictional reflection in Hernando de Soto's self-deifying defiance of his priest at the climax of *At the Moon's Inn.*

After "The Backwoods Progression," Lytle's next major effort in the cause was a long essay in three installments of the *American Review,* dated September, October, and November, 1934. "John Taylor and the Political Economy of Agriculture" was apparently intended for a second symposium that Tate was trying, unsuccessfully, to organize (with T. S. Eliot among the potential contributors). In a prospectus sent to a publisher in November, 1933, Tate lists the following as one of the articles for this proposed book: "Andrew Nelson Lytle: Some Ante-Bellum Planners of Society. Chiefly a discussion of John Taylor of Caroline." The essay that ultimately appeared was entirely a discussion of John Taylor of Caroline (1753–1824), the Virginia philosopher-statesman whose most important works are *The Arator,* a book on agronomy published in 1803, and *An Inquiry into the Prin-*

---

10. Lytle, "Foreword to *A Novel, a Novella and Four Stories,*" in *Hero,* 201.

ciples and Policy of the Government of the United States, an 1814 treatise attacking American materialism. Taylor saw this materialism, which he labeled "the Aristocracy of Paper and Patronage," as a perversion of the independence won from England. Essentially, Lytle portrays Taylor as an Agrarian patriarch, a figure deserving resurrection, given 1930s conditions. The study of American history, Lytle writes, "tells the triumph of senseless greed," and indeed it does when considered, from an Agrarian point of view, as the chronicle of the precipitating actions behind modern society's disorder. Co-opting Taylor for Agrarianism, Lytle venerates him for beginning the fight against the forces of greed in his effort to establish a nation safe for an agrarian, noncapitalistic society. And certainly Taylor, who had been one of the earliest opponents of paper credit, seemed prophetic during the depression years that saw the stock market impoverish many a southern farmer who hardly knew such a thing existed. Lytle's conservatism runs even deeper than Taylor's, though, and he takes occasion to indicate his suspicion of eighteenth-century liberal abstractions like life, liberty, and the pursuit of happiness (whose spirit Taylor caught in youth "as one might catch the pox"). Lytle wrote, "The concern of the leaders of America's revolution should have been, what kind of life? what basis for liberty?—and then there would have been no further need for a pursuit of happiness." [11]

The 1936 essay "The Small Farm Secures the State," whose title encapsulates its thesis, is written out of the same acute awareness of the importance of the concrete texture of life, that is, a healthy mindfulness of man's limitations and fallibility as opposed to any ultimately destructive infatuation with abstract potentiality in whatever form: life, liberty, profit, or progress. Written for *Who Owns America?*—an anti–big business symposium pooling the efforts of southern Agrarians with English Distributists and others—"The Small Farm Secures the State" is in some ways a repeat of "The Hind Tit." Continuing the earlier essay's

11. Tate to Eugene Saxton, November 17, 1933, in Fain and Young (eds.), *Literary Correspondence,* 409–10; Andrew Lytle, "John Taylor and the Political Economy of Agriculture," *American Review,* III (1934), 432, 633; IV (1934), 96.

advocacy of the farmer and his ways, it similarly pauses in mid-polemic to describe in detail the house, orchard, board, and routine of a typical "livelihood farm" (with its negative connotations, "subsistence" is the wrong adjective, says Lytle, for the kind of farm he has in mind). Much more moderate in tone, practical in emphasis, and national in perspective (the South is not mentioned), the later essay is less likely to exasperate the economist and, naturally enough, also less likely to engage the interest of the student of literature. As Louis Rubin has pointed out in *The Wary Fugitives*, the words were rather coldly correct when the ink dried on the Agrarian essays in *Who Owns America?* This symposium played down regional attachment and thus vitiated the passions and pieties that had made *I'll Take My Stand* come alive.[12] In "The Small Farm Secures the State," Lytle is not grappling with the meaning of his southernness or flinging inspired jeremiads in the face of the materialism threatening his inherited culture; instead, he is speaking rather diplomatically in favor of the livelihood farm as part of the answer to national woes. "If our country might boast even one fourth or one third of the population so situated," Lytle writes in a sample passage, "rural life and therefore the life of the nation would by present comparison become wonderfully stable." Back in 1933, with the hope of somehow giving Franklin Roosevelt's incoming administration ideas, Lytle and fellow Agrarian Lyle Lanier had been "working on a program," Lytle wrote Tate, "to get five million people back on the land."[13] One suspects that "The Small Farm Secures the State" was the outgrowth of Lytle's thoughts in that vein. However timely, it was not a particularly rich vein for the imagination.

A much richer vein was the field of fiction, and in the same period that he wrote "The Hind Tit" and "The Small Farm Secures the State," Lytle's earliest fiction also began to appear: three short stories ("Old Scratch in the Valley," "Mr. MacGregor," "Jericho, Jericho, Jericho") and a novel (*The Long Night*). While

12. See Rubin, *The Wary Fugitives*, 253–54.
13. Andrew Lytle, "The Small Farm Secures the State," in Herbert Agar and Allen Tate (eds.), *Who Owns America?* (Boston, 1936), 250; Lytle to Tate, February 23, 1933, in Tate Papers.

Agrarianism as a form of public agitation was coming to an end, the energy Lytle devoted to fiction was growing ever stronger; the novelist in him was pushing aside the cultural commentator. Agrarianism as a movement dissipated soon after the publication of *Who Owns America?* and thus Lytle in 1939 speaks in funereal tones about old Agrarian days. "We had such a grand time," he writes to Frank Owsley, "when all the agrarian brothers were fighting and socializing together. We're scattered, now, for good, I guess. It was a shock for me to get accustomed to acting alone. I don't suppose there has ever been so congenial a literary group nor one which enjoyed itself so well."[14] With Ransom at Kenyon College in Ohio, Warren at Louisiana State University in Baton Rouge, and Tate at the University of North Carolina at Greensboro, and then at Princeton University, the Agrarians were indeed scattered, and it was for good. Yet Lytle has never ceased being an Agrarian in any of the important senses. That is, he has never stopped believing in the broad values that his 1930s Agrarianism posited. Having discovered in the local a heightened image of the universal, he has never tried what probably would have been impossible anyway—to escape his preoccupation with the South.

14. Lytle to Frank Lawrence Owsley, March 23, 1939, in Frank Lawrence Owsley Papers, Special Collections, The Jean and Alexander Heard Library, Vanderbilt University.

IV

From Agrarianism to
Long Gourd Valley

Whereas *Bedford Forrest and His Critter Company* represents Lytle's grasping of his southern heritage, "The Hind Tit" and "The Backwoods Progression," along with the other essays that build on these two, represent the fashioning of that heritage into a weapon. Because the sensibility that infuses Lytle's fiction can hardly disclaim kin with the sensibility that infuses these combative essays, the question arises: has that kinship in any way rendered Lytle's aesthetic parochial? Or, is this adherent of an *ism,* Agrarianism, guilty of sacrificing his taste to the demands of a social thesis? Two of Lytle's earliest stories—"Old Scratch in the Valley" and "Jericho, Jericho, Jericho"—are pertinent texts in this matter, revealing Lytle not simply as the steel-eyed evangel of Agrarianism but as a votary in the service of what Henry James called "felt life."

Published in the *Virginia Quarterly Review* of April, 1932, "Old Scratch in the Valley" is a rather tall short story about the last matriarch of fictive Long Gourd Valley, in turn-of-the-century Middle Tennessee.[1] The story recounts Judith Mebane's feud with Satan over the soul of her Cousin Micajah. When a flood ruins

1. Andrew Lytle, "Old Scratch in the Valley," *Virginia Quarterly Review,* VIII (1932), 237–46, hereinafter cited parenthetically by page number in the text.

Micajah, he blasphemously vows to "build a mill God-a-Mighty can't tear down," and he proceeds to do so despite the out-raged opposition of Judith (243). Judith's matriarchal authority is flouted at every turn, for Micajah uses convict labor to raise his new mill far higher than the river will ever climb. He then de-fiantly enters it on a Sunday to grind the first sack of corn, where-upon he drops dead—struck dead by the Lord, says the commu-nity. Yet even now Judith refuses to give up; she still means to save Micajah for heaven. Gathering together all the family for a funeral without the presence of a clergyman, she prays so long and powerfully over Micajah's coffin that she snatches him from the brink of Hell. As boozing Uncle Jack reports, "The first five minutes, and the devil stopped wagging his tail; the next five and he dropped it beneath his legs like a yaller cur; and by the time she was done you could hear him thrashing his way back to the infernal regions" (246).

No one would make great claims for the story as art, and Lytle chose not to include it in the 1958 collection, *A Novel, a Novella and Four Stories.* Point of view is handled clumsily; the content is self-consciously provincial in the manner of local-color writ-ing; and there is an evasion at the climax, for Judith's miraculous prayer is not rendered even in part. A flawed apprentice piece, this story nonetheless deserves mention. First, it shows Lytle, from the beginning of his career as fiction writer, reaching into the southern past for material—a fundamental characteristic of his literary imagination. ("There is for any Southern writer of imagination," Lytle has written, "an inescapable preoccupation with his native scene and especially with its historic predica-ment.") Second, it is the first instance of a recurrent theme in Lytle's work, the aggrandizement of the individual will; that is, Micajah's license of personal will is a rough prefiguration of a similar element in Kate McCowan in "Jericho, Jericho, Jericho," Pleasant McIvor in *The Long Night,* Hernando de Soto in *At the Moon's Inn,* Henry Brent in *A Name for Evil,* and Pete Legrand in *The Velvet Horn.*[2] Third, "Old Scratch in the Valley" strains to

2. Andrew Lytle, "Regeneration for the Man," in *Hero,* 132. Apropos of McIvor, de Soto, and Brent, see Brewster Ghiselin's discussion of the condition of

some degree under the contrary demands of Agrarian polemics and the Muse.

An obstacle of some concern for an Agrarian desirous of being a novelist, this tension between rhetoric and dramatic rendering shows in a few passages of extraneous commentary grafted onto the narrative. "Long Gourd," Lytle explains in a bit of doctrinaire generalization, "has been very slow to change its way of doing things; and as late as 1910 the people were living as their people had lived, oblivious of and undisturbed by the rapid increase of scientific invention which everywhere else had begun to cut the tap roots of provincial culture" (237). The powerful Mebane family had long been protectors of the Agrarian ordering of this provincial culture, but when Judith, the last Mebane, died, "the framework of Long Gourd society fell apart from the dry rot of an aggravated materialism, and sons and daughters of high-minded individualists lost the sense of independence which had formerly been cultivated as carefully as the valley's fields" (237–38). This passage betrays in the Lytle of 1932 a tendency to lecture about his material rather than to render it, and the excitement of Agrarianism as a fighting cause was partially to blame for this temporary blind spot in Lytle's aesthetic sense.

"Old Scratch in the Valley" is too slight to sustain much analysis, either positive or negative, but with its shortcomings, it makes an instructive contrast with "Jericho, Jericho, Jericho," also set in that first place of Lytle's imagination, Long Gourd Valley (though this time Long Gourd seems to be in northern Alabama). Begun in 1932 but not finished and published till 1936, "Jericho, Jericho, Jericho" skillfully renders what is merely argued in "Old Scratch in the Valley." That is, in depicting the crumbling of the framework of Long Gourd society, it makes no unaesthetic appeal to the reader and contains no ideational top-dressing. In larger terms, the story signifies Lytle's completed journey of the mind from Nashville to Long Gourd, from southern Agrarianism to southern fiction.

"unlimited will": "Andrew Lytle's Selva Oscura," in M. E. Bradford (ed.), *The Form Discovered: Essays on the Achievement of Andrew Lytle* (Jackson, 1973), 74–75.

Widow Kate McCowan, eighty-seven-year-old matriarch of the richest plantation in the valley, is the central character of "Jericho, Jericho, Jericho." The story reveals her in the last hours of her life, *circa* 1930. For seventy years she has poured her vitality into the plantation's four thousand acres, but now she lies beneath the mahogany grapes of the headboard "as dry as any raisin." It is now time, she knows, to yield to the heir, her grandson.

> And here was Long Gourd, all its fields intact, ready to be handed on, in better shape than when she took it over. Yes, she had known what she was doing. How long, she wondered, would his spirit hold up under the trials of planting, of cultivating, and of the gathering time, year in and year out—how would he hold up before so many springs and so many autumns. The thought of him giving orders, riding over the place, or rocking on the piazza, and a great pain would pin her heart to her backbone. She wanted him by her to train—there was so much for him to know: how the creek field was cold and must be planted late, and where the orchards would best hold their fruit, and where the frosts crept soonest.[3]

Dick McCowan, the inheritor, has been called from town to the bedside of his dying grandmother. He is a handsome and well-meaning young man, but his soft hands and "bold, careless face" are perhaps too soft, too careless. As Miss Kate reflects, "He looked a little like his grandpa, but somehow there was something missing" (5). The strange woman with him is a slim beauty he announces as his fiancée, Eva Callahan. "Where'd your folks come from, Eva?" Miss Kate begins. "I knew some Callahans who lived in the Goosepad settlement" (7). Thus is revealed Miss Kate's traditionalistic desire to place this girl within the web of community relationships. But Eva replies:

> "My father and mother live in Birmingham. Have always lived there."

3. Andrew Lytle, "Jericho, Jericho, Jericho," in *A Novel, a Novella and Four Stories* (New York, 1958), 5, 6, hereinafter cited parenthetically by page number in the text. The story was first published in *Southern Review,* 1st ser., I (1936), 753–64.

"Birmingham," she [Miss Kate] heard herself say with contempt. They could have lived there all their lives and still come from somewhere. I've got a mule older'n Birmingham. (8)

In just such subtle details, the omens of conflict, old versus new, reveal themselves.

In private conference with Dick, Miss Kate makes clear her traditionalistic assumptions—what Ransom had termed a persistent regard "for a certain terrain, a certain history, and a certain inherited way of living." She tells her grandson, "You are here to stay, and I'm here to go. There will always be Long Gourd, and there must always be a McCowan on it" (9). As for a wife, she wonders if Dick has picked the right one. "You must forgive the frankness of an old lady who can see the bottom of her grave—I had in mind one of the Carlisle girls. The Carlisle place lies so handy to Long Gourd and would give me a landing on the river. Have you seen Anna Belle since she's grown to be a woman? I'm told there's not a better housekeeper in the valley" (9–10). Miss Kate, as Sidney Landman remarks in his analysis of the story, "sees human relationships not in a romantic light, but in terms of dynastic and communal good." [4]

With her eighteenth-century attitude toward marriage, Miss Kate is not satisfied with Dick's reply that he loves Eva. Romance is not all-sufficient. "She'll wrinkle up on you, Son; and the only wrinkles land gets can be smoothed out by the harrow" (10). Not only would Anna Belle Carlisle have the right dowry, but she would also be a better bet as the dam of future McCowans—a consideration of no small importance in a traditional society. Eva's wasp waist, Miss Kate implies, may compromise her child-bearing abilities. Nonetheless, Miss Kate resigns herself to his choice as best she can, and closes the matter by remarking, "I suppose the safest place for a man to take his folly is to bed" (11).

Then, in deathbed instructions of serious concern to the old

4. John Crowe Ransom, "Reconstructed but Unregenerate," in *I'll Take My Stand: The South and the Agrarian Tradition* (1930; rpr. Baton Rouge, 1977), 1; Sidney J. Landman, "The Walls of Mortality," in Bradford (ed.), *The Form Discovered*, 66.

matriarch, she tells her grandson to be lenient with his Cousin George.

> "He wanders about night times talking about the War. I put him off in the west wing where he won't keep people awake, but sometimes he gets in the yard and gives orders to his troops. 'I will sweep that hill, General'—and many's the time he's done it when the battle was doubtful—'I'll sweep it with my iron brooms'; then he shouts out his orders, and pretty soon the dogs commence to barking. But he's been a heap of company for me. You must see that your wife humors him. It won't be for long. He's mighty feeble."
> (11)

Eva, however, will not be one to take family responsibility so seriously, and neither will Dick. "I was wondering about Cousin George," he replies to his grandmother. "If I could get somebody to keep him. You see, it will be difficult in the winters. Eva will want to spend the winters in town" (11).

Here in these few words is the ruin of the old order, and Miss Kate—dead now in all but pulse and conscience—has a glimpse of this truth. The bed shaking with her agony, she thinks, "Four thousand acres of the richest land in the valley he would sell and squander on that slut, and he didn't even know it and there was no way to warn him" (12). There is no way to warn him not only because her death is imminent and because he is temporarily spellbound by Eva. Already apostate to the *meaning* of those four thousand acres, he no longer has ears to hear. ("You want to say something, Mammy?" he asks in his ignorance as she dies [18].) To think of abandoning Cousin George to strangers, of using Long Gourd for "summering"—such things reveal a man outside the pull of the larger significance of "inheritance." He properly inherits not just a house, but the House of McCowan; not just some acres of dirt and fences, but a complex of responsibilities to place and history, to blood family and servant family. This larger sense of inheritance he renounces, not in a grand gesture (*vide* Ike McCaslin), but in ignorance. He speaks the fateful words, his grandmother rises from the pillow in speechless outrage, and yet he apologizes for nothing more than abusing, he thinks, her stamina ("You must be tired" [11]). Into a "strange newness which does not belong"—to quote from "The Hind Tit"—he has eased unawares.[5]

He has eased out of the Old South traditionalism of Miss Kate and into a new sphere of influence, the New South modernism of fashionable, city-bred Eva.[6] Insofar as they are symbols, Miss Kate betokens the old agrarian order, and Eva—true to her name— the modern fall from order. Dick is the young southerner (the future of the South) at a fulcrum in southern history, a crux between conflicting forces. "Young man," says the attending doctor, "you should feel powerful set up, two such women pestering each other about you" (8). Dick has already chosen the one who glitters, and thus, in terms of the title, it is not only Miss Kate who represents Jericho falling, but it is the traditional South as well. In sum, a larger matrix of events envelops the story and becomes part of its atmosphere. As Allen Tate has observed about Lytle's fiction in general, "The action takes shape out of a vast and turbulent cloud of events, as the funnel of a tornado suddenly forms and descends."[7]

Further, it might be said that the very impulse to write "Jericho, Jericho, Jericho" took shape out of turbulent events, for the story has an arguable relationship to Lytle's Agrarianism. For instance, Miss Kate's devotion to family and tradition seems an Agrarian case in point, and her virtually sacramental view of the plowed earth is exactly that apotheosized in "The Hind Tit." Dick, for his part, suggests a group mentioned in *I'll Take My Stand*'s "Statement of Principles," namely, "younger Southerners, who are being converted frequently to the industrial gospel." And Eva, in all probability, is of that party of urban dwellers who think "that their victuals come from groceries and delicatessens and their milk from tin cans." Such parallels clearly indicate the story's relationship to the particular time and place of its origin.[8]

5. Andrew Lytle, "The Hind Tit," in *I'll Take My Stand,* 245.

6. Sidney Landman, too, sees the story as "a parable of the fall of the South." See "The Walls of Mortality," in Bradford (ed.), *The Form Discovered,* 64.

7. Allen Tate, Foreword to Lytle, *Hero,* xiv.

8. "Statement of Principles," in *I'll Take My Stand,* xxxviii; Lytle, "The Hind Tit," in *ibid.,* 203.

However, to see "Jericho, Jericho, Jericho" in a propagandistic alliance with Agrarianism would be an oversimplification. There *is* an alliance, but it is not propagandistic. With her reverence for land and family, Miss Kate may have the outlines of a candidate for Agrarian canonization, but Lytle does not confer sainthood. The story is hardly so simple as that; indeed, it is rich in ambiguities. The third-person limited point of view reveals the story's other characters only through Miss Kate's eyes, and in the way she reacts to others, the shadows of her character come to deepen the picture. She has a grasping, sinful—in other words thoroughly human—side.

For instance, before Eva has spoken a word, Miss Kate silently judges her to be "standing by the bed as if she owned it" (6). Whatever the look on Eva's face, Miss Kate interprets it with a thought strongly suggesting her sense of proprietorship, her own rather fierce sense of *mine.* When Eva stutters, "I wanted to come and see—to meet Dick's grandmother," Miss Kate thinks to herself, "*I wanted to come see her die.* That's what she meant. Why didn't she finish and say it out. She had come to lick her chops and see what she would enjoy. That's what she had come for, the lying little slut" (7). Miss Kate may well be right (it would have a symbolic aptness), but one cannot help noting how uncharitably predisposed she is to just such a judgment. And her sense of possession extends with a kind of jealousy even to her grandson, for her eyes burn as they travel over "the woman who would lie in her bed, eat with her silver, and caress her flesh and blood" (7). The jealousy of one who is dying toward those who will survive is a part of the tangle of emotions behind her bitterness toward Eva and her pain at the thought of Dick "giving orders, riding over the place, or rocking on the piazza" (6).

Beyond loving too well what she must leave 'ere long, however, is an act Miss Kate fears as her damnation. As she orders Dick from the room, her foreknowledge of Long Gourd's fall sharp in her mind, "the specter of an old sin rose up to mock her" (12). A scene from the past plays through her mind once again: years before she had annexed neighboring property under equivocal circumstances. She hears the old voices:

> "You promised Pa to look after me"—she [Kate] had waited for the voice to break and scream—"and you have stolen my land!"
>
> "Now, Miss Iva Louise," the lawyer dropped his empty eyes along the floor, "you don't mean . . ."
>
> "Yes. I do mean it."
>
> Her own voice had restored calm to the room: "I promised your pa his land would not be squandered." (12)

By taking over the defaulted tax payments of Iva Louise's inherited property, Miss Kate had perhaps kept it from being squandered by Iva Louise's good-for-nothing husband, but her motives were impure. Even now she wonders, "Had she stolen the land because she wanted it?" (13). The answer, at least in part, is yes, and her present torment—Dick and Eva's imminent betrayal of Long Gourd—is her punishment, the wheel come round again. The "trapped look" on Iva Louise's face "had come back to her, now trapped in her bed" (13).

Thus Miss Kate is not a one-dimensional Agrarian heroine, and neither is the old order the stuff of impossible legend or propagandistic unimpeachability. The representative of an older day, Miss Kate is powerless to ensure that her way of life is continued. To the degree that she is a symbol of the old provincial establishment, that establishment by extension appears admirable but powerless to perpetuate itself—hardly a sign of a virile culture. Is this traditional culture implicated in its own demise? Assuredly its center will not hold, and not solely because of outside forces.

Cousin George, a Civil War veteran still wandering the thickets of some Shiloh in his mind, also represents a surviving element of the traditional culture. His character is well glossed by the words of the southern statesman and editor Walter Hines Page.

> I have sometimes thought that many of the men who survived that unnatural war unwittingly did us a greater hurt than the war itself. It gave every one of them the intensest experience of his life and ever afterward he referred every other experience to this. Thus it

> stopped the thought of most of them as an earthquake stops a
> clock. The fierce blows of battle paralyzed the mind. Their speech
> was a vocabulary of war, their loyalties were loyalties, not to living
> ideas or duties, but to old commanders and to distorted traditions.
> They were dead men, most of them, moving among the living as
> ghosts.[9]

His mind paralyzed by the blows of battle, Cousin George wanders Long Gourd like a ghost, and the only troops answering his
orders now are the dogs. He has never recovered from the shock
of military defeat and thus spends his hours in contemplation of
the Lost Cause. Lost to the present because he is lost in the past,
he is—to extend his significance—the symptom of a culture's
decline.

In view of the deterioration of the old order, Dick's readiness
to desert Cousin George and Long Gourd, though not excusable,
is at least understandable. No matter how ruinous Eva may in the
end turn out to be, she has life, youth, magnetism. The temptations of modernism—cars, sophistication, the lure of easy
money—all take place offstage in "Jericho, Jericho, Jericho," and
we are not told, for instance, what attracted Dick to town. But
Eva perhaps reflects those temptations. She is indeed tempting
with her "firm, round breasts," her "lips, full and red," and "her
eyes bright and cunning" (7). The debasement of southern tradition is a central theme in "Jericho, Jericho, Jericho," but Lytle
gives it a rich, life-imitating complexity. The conflict of old versus new is not a simple matter of unmitigated good versus unmitigated bad.

This complexity reflects the difference between a South-
defending Agrarian novelist and a novelist who happens also to
be a southern Agrarian—the difference between the hot patriot
and the cool artist. "Jericho, Jericho, Jericho" does not depend
for effect on an assumption that its audience nurtures specifically
southern or Agrarian pieties. Whereas the intrusive commentary
in "Old Scratch in the Valley" largely depends for effect on the

9. Quoted in Burton J. Hendrick, *The Life and Letters of Walter Hines Page*
(New York, 1923), I, 90–91.

satisfaction of finding one's beliefs echoed, "Jericho, Jericho, Jericho" relies on no such extraliterary appeal. By letting his story's imagined world in a sense reveal itself (through the third-person limited point of view), Lytle keeps his own shadow out of the picture.[10] This approach is what Henry James called the born novelist's "respect unconditioned for the freedom and vitality, the absoluteness when summoned, of the creatures he invokes." As Lytle himself stated in a review of William Faulkner's *Intruder in the Dust*:

> It is the writer's nature to discover for himself his meaning by matching his knowledge of experience against his imagination. This never comes in a burst of light, but out of a gradual exploration into the dark places of the mind and heart of man. The process of writing forces the discovery; or rather it is the discovery. What saves the writer from losing himself (the points of darkness are infinite) is his point of view. To this he may return and by this he may relate, reduce, and absorb the seemingly unrelated matters of experience until they become what to him is truth.[11]

By fusing the rational and the intuitive in the crucible of art— that is, by "matching his knowledge of experience against his imagination"—Lytle wrote a story not didactic but dramatic. Therefore, even though "Jericho, Jericho, Jericho" pondered an Agrarian subject and was written when Agrarianism was still alive as a fighting cause, the story is not hamstrung by any extraneous concern with social action, by any hint of doctrine.

This fidelity to the dictates of the imagination is relevant in another respect as well. Anyone who has read Lytle's "family his-

10. The danger of letting the shadow intrude is well expressed in this passage from an essay Lytle published in 1959: "Opinion is the vulgarity of taste. It is never a true idea, because it is either topical or partial. It distorts any action, since it is blind to the fullest complexity of that action. No matter how disguised, opinion always has a 'message,' it always wants to prove something instead of making experience show itself." From "the Working Novelist and the Myth-making Process," in *Hero*, 181.

11. Henry James, "Ivan Turgenieff," in M. D. Zabel (ed.), *The Portable Henry James* (New York, 1968), 457; Lytle, "Regeneration for the Man," in *Hero*, 132–33.

tory of a region," *A Wake for the Living,* will notice the lineaments of Lytle's grandmother, Kate Lytle, and his great-grandmother, Judith Lytle, in the fictional Kate McCowan (and also in the matriarch of "Old Scratch in the Valley," Judith Mebane). For instance, Judith Lytle epitomized "the last of the Southern matriarchy," and Kate Lytle had that "family pride which you find only where the family is attached to the land and remains attached." [12] Although by no means thinly disguised biography, "Jericho, Jericho, Jericho" was nonetheless a meditation on Lytle's own family heritage. By "matching his knowledge of experience against his imagination" and exploring "the dark places of the mind and heart of man," Lytle was able to transmute this meditation into a work with rich, more-than-personal meaning.

"Jericho, Jericho, Jericho" is the fully realized work of a man in control of his craft, and it shows Lytle's dedication not to a narrow defense of the South per se, but to the artistically purer goal of fidelity to his imagination, wherever it leads. That the story reveals Lytle's maturation as an artist should not be surprising, for it was preceded by nine years of preparatory work: the workshop under George Pierce Baker, the writing of *Bedford Forrest* and several unpublished plays, all the Agrarian activities, the trial flight of "Old Scratch in the Valley," the fuller flight of "Mr. MacGregor," and, finally, the two years of hammering away at *The Long Night.* In "Jericho, Jericho, Jericho," Lytle draws on his inheritance in a way quite different from "The Hind Tit." He successfully makes the transition from the disputatious world of Agrarianism to the subtler world of Long Gourd Valley—yet he retains all the while what is best and broadest in Agrarianism.

12. Lytle, *A Wake for the Living,* 205, 8. See also 195, 199, 205–207, 213.

V

Old Times in the Coosa Country
The Long Night

When Lytle's first novel, *The Long Night*, came out in September, 1936, Allen Tate noted its "prodigality of material," its "seven or eight main episodes," any of which "could have been expanded into a full-length novel." This prodigality is not a defect, maintained Tate, for each episode both carries the story forward and enriches it. What the story is enriched with, the social texture of the southern past, is an indication of the nature of Lytle's imagination and is also the reason this violent, at times melodramatic narrative of revenge has an affinity, surprisingly enough, with the novel of manners. Lytle gives his scene, up-country Alabama before Civil War defeat, a density and complexity in which we can know the characters by their habits and stations, as they know each other—the Campbellite by his piety, the Kentuckian by his scorn for King Cotton, the proud planter by his diction or even his black slippers, the no less proud yeoman by his broad-brimmed hat, or the poor white by his soiled smock and bad grammar. The material of *The Long Night*, Robert Penn Warren has said,

> sprang from the world that always most stirred Andrew's imagination and humor. He knew the world of the plantation and of the

deeper backcountry in the hills beyond the plantations. He knew the language, every shade of it by tone and phrase, every inflection, every hint of pain or poetry, the humor, the bawdiness, every expression of face. He knew the objects and practices of the old times, and of the backcountry, how meat was dressed, how food was cooked, how meal was ground or hominy made, what people— men or women or children—wore, how wool was carded, how shakes were split and whiskey run. He knew such things because he had the keenest of eyes, the shrewdest of ears, insatiable curiosity, and an elephantine memory; but mostly because he had a natural generosity and simplicity of heart and could stop a stranger on the road or lounge on the steps of the most desolate crossroads store and in ten minutes be swapping crop-talk or tales with the local whittlers, in perfect ease and pleasure and with devoted attention.

Lytle's fascination with the character of his historic inheritance— a fascination first evident in *Bedford Forrest and His Critter Company*—brings a rich particularity to *The Long Night* that is not a matter of background merely, for in a significant way it directs the meaning of the novel.[1]

The opening chapter of *The Long Night* introduces the ostensible author, Lawrence McIvor. Fresh from college and about to marry, he receives what seems a "communication from another world," a letter from an uncle long presumed dead.[2] Pleasant McIvor's curiously peremptory note directs his homeward-bound nephew to stop first in Winston County in the hills of northern Alabama. Deep in the wilderness cove that is his uncle's retreat, Lawrence, dripping in cold sweat, hears the old man's story of vengeance. It is near the turn of the century as the two sit all night before the hearth, but the dark tale that unfolds harks back to the years from 1859 to 1862.

1. Allen Tate, "A Prodigal Novel of Pioneer Alabama," *Books,* September 6, 1936, p. 3; Robert Penn Warren, "Andrew Lytle's *The Long Night:* A Rediscovery," *Southern Review,* n.s., VII (1971), 132–33. On the novel's "fullness," see also H. L. Weatherby, "The Quality of Richness: Observations on Andrew Lytle's *The Long Night,*" in Bradford (ed.), *The Form Discovered,* 35–41.

2. Andrew Lytle, *The Long Night* (New York, 1936), 14, hereinafter cited parenthetically by page number in the text.

The events of Pleasant's tale begin in Wetumpka, Alabama, when Cameron McIvor, Pleasant's father, is murdered in bed by the pawns of a slave- and mule-stealing network headed by a man named Tyson Lovell. In his desperate grief young Pleasant locks himself in a room, where for two days and nights he prays and rages. He emerges strangely changed, a monomaniac committed to reprisal not just against the three men who killed his father but also against the forty or more who were behind the murder. From all over the South, the McIvor clan draws together in secret council and settles upon a course of action: revenge must be exacted not in open feud but in stealth. Pleasant and a few others will be the avengers.

Then the bodies begin to fall. The corrupt judge is kicked from the Coosa Inn balcony, one Wilton brother is dragged to death by his horse, the other appears to have shot himself while cleaning his gun, and so on—more than thirteen killings. When the Civil War erupts, Pleasant joins the Confederate ranks, for under cover of the southern cause he can hunt his scattered quarry through every company of the army. While soldiering, though, the cold revenger is gradually warmed by comradeship and a sense of public duty. He fights at Shiloh and Perryville, all the while avoiding and even at times forgetting his vow of vengeance. On a scouting mission in the fall of 1862, he tries one last time to revive the old hatred, but, taking aim before the sleeping figure of one of his father's murderers, he cannot pull the trigger. However, having thus postponed his return to headquarters with important information, Pleasant learns that this delay has meant death for his friend Roswell, who could have led him back into the world of community ties. Shattered, Pleasant deserts not only the army, but life itself. "In the secret coves, far away from the world and vengeance, a deserter might hide forever" (331).

The story is an antirevenge revenge tragedy in the mode of many Elizabethan plays, the best known being Thomas Kyd's *The Spanish Tragedy* and William Shakespeare's *Hamlet.* Like that of Hieronymo and Hamlet, Pleasant's violent resolve taints his soul; thus Lytle's novel shows revenge to be morally reprehensible because of the way it distorts the character of the hero. We perhaps cheer Pleasant on to his bloody deeds at first, but Lytle gradually makes us feel the chill as Pleasant becomes cold-blooded. His self-appointment to the role of divine avenger is enormously presumptuous; he claims that he "hears" his dead father, calls himself "God's judgment" (187), and quotes Old Testament vindictiveness ("I have pursued mine enemies and overtaken them; neither did I return again until they were consumed" [217]). But the book makes clear that he would do better to ponder the New Testament, for instance, Paul to the Romans: "Avenge not yourselves, but rather give place unto wrath: for it is written, Vengeance is mine; I will repay, saith the Lord." [3]

I do not intend to suggest that Lytle was consciously working from Elizabethan models in shaping the meaning of *The Long Night*. As Robert Penn Warren has pointed out and as Lytle's correspondence amply substantiates, the immediate prototype for Pleasant was the real-life "Uncle Dink" of Lytle's friend Frank Owsley. In the summer of 1933, while visiting Cornsilk, Owsley told Lytle the tale of his great-uncle, who, like Pleasant, had devoted himself to avenging the gang murder of his father. For Owsley's old relative, though, the mission of revenge never grew stale, and it was not out of guilt, bluster, or moral admonition that he told his nephew his story. Rather, growing old and weak, he felt the need to pass the bloody obligation on to his kinsman, for two or three of the murderers were still above ground. [4]

In short, the narrative Lytle appropriated from Owsley had nothing to do with the moral ambiguities of revenge. It was simply an uncomplicated, essentially heroic story about a rather awe-inspiring eccentric until Lytle began to shape the raw substance of life into art. Sinking himself into the task of creation and wrestling with the matter of Owsley's family tale, he saw *The Long Night* change from a heroic memorialization of Owsley's Uncle Dink to something darker and richer. Thus Lytle explained

3. Rom. 12:19.
4. See Warren, "Andrew Lytle's *The Long Night*," 130–39; Owsley to Lytle, October 3, 1936, in Lytle Papers. The Lytle-Owsley correspondence makes clear that the old man was passing the task of revenge down to Frank Owsley's father, not—as Warren misstates it—to Frank Owsley himself.

to Owsley, one month after the novel's publication, that "the biography of your Uncle Dink and [the] novel I was doing had turned out to be different things. . . . the novel became more a story of this semi-pioneer community and less the story of Uncle Dink."[5] That is, the social background against which Pleasant's acts of vengeance take place, the *mise-en-scène*, assumed greater and greater emphasis until it became a sprawling depiction of the world through which Pleasant's victims move, serving to reveal his loss of humanity in stark relief. Lytle's portrayal of the texture of Old Southwest society shapes the meaning of the novel by throwing Pleasant's obsession into its true, tragic light.

Of the book's five chapters, Chapter 3, composing almost half of the novel's bulk, demonstrates this function of social texture most fully. Chapter 1 provides the book's frame, the artifice of Lawrence going to hear his old uncle's tale, and Chapter 2 provides the background, an exposition of the events culminating in Cameron McIvor's murder. Chapter 4, which deals at length with the battle of Shiloh, sees the avenger carry his will to revenge into the Civil War, where it begins to give way before new allegiances. Chapter 5 swiftly records the tragic conclusion—the beloved friend dead and Pleasant, seeing himself in tragic clarity, indirectly to blame. The central thread of Chapter 3, however, unlike that of any other chapter, is the exacting of revenge. Special attention is given to the dispatching of Judge Wilton, Dee Day, Damon Harrison, and Sheriff Botterall, as well as to Pleasant's confrontation with the evil kingpin, Tyson Lovell. A rudimentary indication of the interplay between the action of revenge and the delineation of old times in the South is that in this 133-page chapter plotted on vengeance nearly 60 pages have nothing to do, strictly speaking, with the pursuit or atmosphere of revenge. With its love affairs, wakes, pigeon jugging, beekeeping, horse training, and yarn swapping, the commonplace life of the Buyckville community swells out of the narrative and subtly conditions our response to Pleasant.

5. Lytle to Owsley, in Owsley Papers. Dated only "Wednesday evening," but clearly a reply to a letter Owsley wrote on October 3, 1936.

Lytle's treatment of Damon Harrison, one of Pleasant's victims, is a good example of this rich particularity, for Damon is not a flat character whose blood is let to reader applause. As he does for almost all those who die, Lytle gives a number of vignettes from the marked man's life. Thus we get to know Damon as a human being, as a youth just coming into manhood, not just as a target for righteous revenge. The Damon we get to know is overbred and high-strung, naïve and impetuous—and has gotten into bad company—but he is not at all despicable.

That Damon is the son of low-country aristocrats is an important part of his character, and Lytle's depiction of Harrison family history is one of the novel's most effective prodigalities. Quintus Harrison, now proprietor of Buyckville's crossroads store, had once been the third-generaton master of Fair Meadows, a grand plantation in low-country Alabama. But one Sunday when Damon was ten, his hot-blooded father, while shooting taws, gambled away land, slaves, mansion, indeed, his whole inheritance. It is a well-rendered little drama—Quintus looking up from Edmund Burke's orations to greet his neighbor, the friendly game begun, the high words exchanged, and then, all unknowing, Damon's mother coming upon the scene of catastrophe.

> Quint was sitting quietly in his rocker when his wife returned from the quarters.
> "I think old Eph will be all right now, though I'm afraid of pneumonia." She hesitated.
> "What's the matter, Mr. Harrison? You are pale. Are you sick too?"
> "You needn't trouble yourself about Ephraim any more." Her husband's voice seemed to drag out forever. "He belongs to Malcolm Buford."
> She looked at Quintus for further explanation, but he was unable to answer her. Damon burst out excitedly:
> "Mama, papa's just shot away all the niggers and Fair Meadows."
> For some seconds the words had no meaning and then suddenly she knew it was true. Thirty minutes ago she had walked away from the house, mistress of two thousand acres of land and seventy servants. On her return . . . she knew it was true because it was more real than life. The fatal words rang upon her ears as if she had heard them over many times. The time, the place, the position of

her husband and son on the piazza seemed familiar like a con-
stantly recurring dream. (122)

The Harrisons move north to the up-country, where Quintus,
ever courteous, formal, and aloof, sets up business only to distance himself from it as much as possible. His customers make
their own change and their own year-end settlements, and even
"hand him things to take to the house for his wife" (110). His tall
wife, for her part, exists in a constant state of outrage and near
madness, punishing her husband by cramming the dining room
of their little dog-run house with the oppressive evidence of the
past and their former station. Crowding the humble room are
silver candelabra, a mahogany banquet table, a massive side-
board, and the reproachful faces of over a dozen family portraits.
The house smells of lye, its floors worn with scouring. "Don't
you think, my dear," says Quintus, "it's a little hard on the ser-
vants to use so much water this dry weather?" She replies, "You
know, Mr. Harrison, the poor white smells of this house give me
asthma" (117).

Such is Damon's family situation, and he is resentful of what he
considers his mother's "lack of courage in the face of misfor-
tune. . . . how she had made this cabin her shell, never leaving it,
pretending the up-country had no existence" (118). Growing up
in this backcountry and feeling himself driven into rebellion,
Damon draws away from his mother and "into the hill life about
him" (123). He seeks out the wildest companions, while his
mother, more aware than her pretending suggests, waits in dread
for disaster. Thus Damon's association with an unsavory element
of Buyckville society is part of a complex series of events and
relationships; he is not just some shadowy ruffian, some simple
convenience within a plot appealing merely to the base emotions associated with revenge.

Damon frolics with the Wiltons, who are criminals in Lovell's
employ, and he rides with the posse that kills Cameron McIvor.
But it is never plain whether he is knowingly party to Lovell's
evil machinations or is simply among those deluded into thinking that old Cameron, framed and outlawed, is a slave-stealing
abolitionist and thus a threat to the community (the time is

1859, soon after the John Brown raid). However ignoble, acting out of a communal sense of self-preservation is different from willful, cynical criminality. When Pleasant later confronts him at knife-point, Damon refers to Pleasant's dead father as "that old son-of-a-bitching nigger stealer," which suggests that Damon is part of the duped community at large, not one of Lovell's creatures (172). It is a flaw in the narrative, though, that this is not made completely clear.

Damon, for all his swaggering, is not without sympathetic qualities. There is his courage, for instance, in breaking a wild mule, and his youthful ache when suddenly enamored of one of the neighborhood girls as she races, bell lifted, after an escaping swarm of bees. Damon enjoys just those things that Pleasant's obsession precludes—camaraderie, community life, young love. Damon is a foil to Pleasant, as is Roswell Ellis later in the story, and by contrast each shows the desolation of Pleasant's chosen path (and the irony of his name). The implied contrast is at no time clearer than when, in the forest outside the Weaver house, Damon and Ruth feel the tender promise of first love, while, ever roaming the dark like an animal, Pleasant stalks them. His mere presence charges the air of the woods, at first "friendly and comforting," with a "feeling of fear and hate," as nature, not sinister in itself, answers to the malevolence of the human heart (171). Suddenly, Pleasant's violence shatters the lovers' idyll. "You've made enough noise, Damon Harrison, to wake the dead. . . . But you'll never raise Cameron McIvor from his grave" (172). Stabbed, Damon bleeds to death in Ruth's arms; Pleasant nurses his wounds alone. Then, to close the Harrison subplot, the novel reveals the father in sorrow, carrying his son into the house, and the mother, as she washes the pale body and combs the hair, relenting in her hate and hardness.

One of the effects of knowing the Harrisons is to thwart easy acceptance of Pleasant's eye-for-an-eye ethic. The pathos of Damon's death serves to underscore the ambiguities of Pleasant's character, as does the depiction of all the bustling life of the Buyckville neighborhood, from country feasting, judging of horseflesh, and rough humor to the women's sharing of recipes and troubles. Lytle purposely undercuts the momentum of the revenge plot and, in a sense, the justice of Pleasant's bloody deeds by slowing the pace again and again, with a storefront anecdote here, a life history there. At the wake for Alf Weaver and Brother Macon, for instance, the women shake their heads and discuss their "fool men." Her husband, Mrs. Botterall laments, recently came home drunk and hitched his mare to the bedpost. "I got in bed with mammy," she says, "but I couldn't sleep. Who could sleep with him a-snoren drunk and the mare a-tromping and you know what in my bedroom?" Then ancient Aunt Patsy, once an Indian captive and a survivor of two husbands, takes out her pipe and joins the litany. "I buried two of'm. The fust one—it was sw'are, sw'are, sw'are. The last one—pra'er, pra'er, pra'er" (160).

Such comic vignettes, drawn from the family and community world from which Pleasant has distanced himself, dissolve the reader's temptation to endorse his mania. As Robert Penn Warren has said, "Bit by bit, the reader's attention is shifted from the story of the avenger, Pleasant McIvor, to the common, daylight life of the community." Even the villains, asserts Warren, become "merely men, certainly no better than they should be, but trapped somehow in their destiny. Whose side are we on? This doubleness of view, and the irony it entails, is a fundamental fact of the story as it appears in the novel."[6] Warren cites the comic shrouding of Brother Macon as an effective example of Lytle's rendering of the common life of the community. Abner Buchanan, a Baptist who has always enjoyed baiting the Campbellite Brother Macon, learns that his friends have saved for him the job of scrubbing Macon's corpse. Boisterous from the bottled cheer making the rounds of the room, Buchanan announces that he is ready.

> Beatty and Simmons drew back the sheet.
> "Where do you want him, Ab?"
> Abner stepped back unsteadily and looked at the body.
> "Well, now, you've got me stumped. I'm new to this kind of a trade."
> "Somebody git the wash tub," growled Botterall.

6. Warren, "Andrew Lytle's *The Long Night*," 136–37.

"You ain't figgering for me to set him in the tub, Lem?"

"Hell, no. But what's to keep you from standen him up in it?"

"That's an idey. I deputize you to hold, sheriff."

"You can't deshutize the sheriff."

"That's a fact. Well, Joe, you hold him."

Joe looked at the corpse.

"He'll lean ag'in the wall," he said.

The tub was brought, and the corpse of Brother Macon, after the clothes had been clumsily stripped, was lifted in. At this moment Damon returned with another bucket of water. He saw the grayish-brown figure leaning grotesquely against the mantelpiece. . . .

"Here's the other bucket of water. Be enough?"

"A bucket of water? Dump it in the tub, my boy," Abner said gaily, rolling up his sleeves.

Damon's face lost its color and he hesitated; but, looking down, he did as he was told. He could not help but see the water splash around the still, ashen legs. As soon as he had emptied the pail, he picked up the other one and left the room.

"The boy's got weak guts," said Beatty pleasantly.

"That's a sight to turn stronger guts to jelly," answered Botterall. The assistants began to look a little grim.

"You boys ain't white-eyed on me?" Abner asked cheerfully.

"Hell, no," said Beatty. "He won't bite."

"Pitch the soap in that ar bucket and swing out the pot."

It was done in silence, and Buchanan picked up the broom. He dipped it in the kettle and swung the scalding water on the corpse.

"Ain't you a-goen to mix the water?"

"If it's too hot fer'm, he'll holler."

He ran the broom into the water, over the soap, then over the legs of the corpse.

"'Y God," he said, "but I believe the dirt's set on him." (162–63)

Finally, with Brother Macon washed and dressed, even his hair combed, Buchanan solemnly declares, "Well, here's one Campbellite that'll be buried a Christian" (164). Buchanan's helpers—Botterall, Beatty, and Simmons—are three of the villains Pleasant will kill, but their comicality heightens the reader's sensitivity to the ambiguities of revenge.

In further remarking the novel's handling of scene, Warren especially emphasizes Lytle's skill in conveying a sharp impression of this society and its history through the accurately transcribed talk of its people. For instance, a young wife who maintains that her husband, even after the birth of their child, has not fallen off in his attentions receives the reply, "You're eaten yore white bread now" (159). As Warren points out, the analogy behind these words invokes a context that opens a deeper glimpse into this semifrontier world. She is baking with white flour now, but in time she will be eating the coarser, darker bread made from the bran and tailings at the bottom of the barrel.[7]

Complicating the reader's initial identification with the McIvor revenge code, Lytle's rich delineation of this up-country Alabama world brings irony to the action of revenge. This daylight world was the same one Pleasant enjoyed before his youth was violated by tragedy, but now he skulks through the night, hides in the hills, sleeps in caves; the only fellowship he shares is with the "voice" of his dead father. We come to worry not so much about Pleasant's physical safety as his moral safety. If, for instance, we do not much lament the passing of Sheriff Botterall, neither do we feel comfortable with Pleasant's satisfaction in having Botterall cut to pieces by the plunging hooves of a wild stallion. As is clear in the case of Damon Harrison, coming to know the victims and their everyday milieu does not uniformly make it easy to watch them die. Further, coming to know Pleasant does not make it easy to watch him kill.

Especially in the climactic scene of Chapter 3, in which Pleasant confronts Tyson Lovell, the dubiety of Pleasant's moral position is clearly intimated—and not wholly by indirection, as in the earlier renderings of social texture. Slipping into Lovell's pitch-black office at nightfall, Pleasant hears a satanic voice emerge from the darkness: "I've been expecting you" (185). Neither man can see the other, and the man Lovell expected and thinks he addresses is someone else, a hired assassin with bloodhounds for tracking Pleasant. Lovell's words, though, are eerily appropriate all the same. "Is your name . . . ," begins Pleasant, only to be interrupted with, "Your business is not names. Your busi-

7. *Ibid.,* 136–37, 135.

ness is blood. . . . Where are your hounds? The bloody dogs of
Hell" (186). Then finally, when each knows whom he faces and
Pleasant has given his enemy two minutes to prepare for death,
Lovell asks pointedly, "what will you do, sonny, when I'm dead
and gone?" (187). Indeed, what else is there for Pleasant? His humanity has shriveled in the darkness of his long night of revenge
(thus the trenchant irony of his being mistaken for his own assassin), and his monomania has so reduced his being that he is
nothing more than his one purpose.

"In the whole wide world," says Lovell, "there are no two men
so filled with grit as you and I. . . . together we might corrupt
Hell" (189). Indeed, no matter how honorable Pleasant may
think his motives are, he has become damnably similar to his adversary. In this light, earlier descriptions of the snakelike, gliding,
sudden-striking avenger take on Luciferian undertones (see 105,
136, 177). It is interesting, too, that when Pleasant walks toward
the dogtrot of Lovell's house, described as a gravelike "mouth
gaping in the dark . . . he knew that he was being led, led in
his doubting moment" (183). Pleasant imagines always that it is
Providence guiding him safely along the path of retribution, but
we have reason to wonder otherwise. In a sense, presuming to
know God's purpose is a dangerous elevation of private will. Further, the otherworldly force drawing Pleasant on has certainly
not done his soul any good. In answering evil with evil, Pleasant
has inevitably suffered a moral rot. One thinks, for instance, of
his blanket-mate's symbolic nightmare, later in the war section of
the book. "From where I thought you lay," reports Roswell, "the
smell of corruption rose thick and stifling, two long bony arms
reached about my waist, with hot rotting chunks of flesh falling,
and wherever they fell scalding me" (324).

Pleasant does not kill Lovell, however. Learning of the Civil
War's eruption, which has dashed the gang leader's dream of empire, Pleasant postpones killing him so that Lovell can anguish in
the knowledge of failure and the threat of ever-hovering doom.
Pleasant joins the Army of Tennessee, at first still bent on revenge. "He could not help thinking what good luck the war had
brought, gathering his enemies in such confusion in the pres-

ence of his vengeance" (203). He gradually begins to notice, though, that his thoughts are drifting from his private obsession and turning instead to the public effort to drive out the northern invaders. Cousin Armistead McIvor, earlier a partner in revenge but now a Confederate colonel, tells him that it is "every Southern man's duty to put away his private life now," and Pleasant discovers with some amazement that he can "sleep like other men," raise the rebel yell, thrill at the sight of the battle flag, and even feel friendship (224). During the furious violence of Shiloh, he, the impassive avenger who has supp'd full with horrors, suddenly feels a terrible nausea at the smell of blood, the sight of death, the awful waste.[8] Lying down to drink from a pond, for instance, he finds the water bloody and all the other drinkers frozen in rigor mortis. Faint, he pulls away in revulsion. Then, in the rainy dusk, he and a wounded Federal help each other boil coffee. In short, in the great cataclysm of the war, Pleasant regains his humanity. "His old life with its clear sure purpose lay somewhere lost in this confusion, and he would never reach it again" (306).

Tragically, Pleasant makes a final effort to recover his old life. His brothers William and Levi having died soon after the Kentucky campaign, Pleasant meets his mother when she comes to take her sons' bodies home, and the presence of the still-bitter widow pains him with "the knowledge that he had turned aside." (316). Her eyes say to him: "these I have lost, but you are left, and I could better lose them both than you, for my oldest and my youngest have wasted themselves on foolish adventures. You will never turn away and spend yourself on things that do not matter" (315). Soon after, on a scout, he notes an enemy concentration near LaVergne but delays making his report so that he

8. Lytle's handling of the battle of Shiloh has been praised by such commentators as Allen Tate, Louis Rubin, and Walter Sullivan. See, respectively, "A Prodigal Novel of Pioneer Alabama," 3; "The Image of an Army," in *The Curious Death of the Novel: Essays in American Literature* (Baton Rouge, 1967), 197; "Southern Novelists and the Civil War," in Louis D. Rubin, Jr., and Robert D. Jacobs (eds.), *Southern Renascence: The Literature of the Modern South* (Baltimore, 1953), 117–19.

can exact yet another revenge. He aims the pistol, then lowers it. "Shivering with nausea and the cold, he accepted the truth: it was not in him any longer to kill in cold blood" (327). Allegiance to the southern cause and affection for his comrades, especially for his friend Roswell Ellis, have "taken him as the flood current takes the great tree, torn up by its roots" (327). But when he returns to camp, Roswell is nowhere to be found. He is dead, Pleasant learns, killed at LaVergne in an action that Pleasant's information, discovered thirty-six hours earlier, would have prevented. "As a mourner before the open grave Pleasant dropped his head to the ground, where Roswell should be sleeping, waiting, and the ground was empty, as empty as his heart. Then suddenly he knew what he had done, what no man in this world may do. Twice he had loved—once the dead, once the living, and each by each was consumed and he was doomed" (330).

To this has revenge brought him. The angel of death for so many, he has now borne death to his friend and death-in-life to himself. With self-knowledge he retreats to the hills of Winston a ruined human being, but at least a human being. That the reader recognizes the dehumanizing nature of Pleasant's devotion to vengeance long before he himself recognizes it is partially a function of the novel's enrichment with what Lytle termed the "story of this semi-pioneer community." Thus Lytle's feel for the community past of his region helps shape the meaning as well as the setting of his revenge tragedy.

VI

Moon-Madness in the New World and the Southern Roots of
At the Moon's Inn

At the Moon's Inn, published in 1941, Lytle's second novel, tells
the story of Hernando de Soto's expedition into the Florida ter-
ritory, beginning with the Adelantado's mesmerizing of gold-
hungry recruits in Spain and ending with the secret sinking of his
corpse in the Mississippi River. In shining breastplates, de Soto
and his soldiers march ashore on the Gulf coast of Florida in
1539. Then, through swamp and forest, they struggle north in
hope of finding such gold as de Soto had found in Peru. Instead,
however, they find only the maize of tribe after proud tribe. Although they soon learn to see the maize as a kind of treasure (for
starving men), it cannot satisfy the relentless de Soto, who steadily reveals just how far he has become food for "the two worms
in the forked tongue of Satan," avarice and pride.[1] When the conquistadors reach the earthly paradise of Cutifichiqui in present-
day South Carolina, they do find a burial temple replete with
pearls. Here, also, many of the Spaniards take Indian paramours.
Discovering that the sea is only two days distant, the men are

---

1. Andrew Lytle, *At the Moon's Inn* (New York, 1941), 56, hereinafter cited
parenthetically by page number in the text.

ready to colonize, but the Adelantado drives the army westward, the fabled gold always sure to be just over the horizon. After a pyrrhic victory over Indians at the battle of Mauvilla (near present-day Mobile, Alabama), the pacification of La Tierra Florida becomes demoralized wandering, the army now dressed in skins and held together only by the willpower of de Soto. Finally, after a time of increasingly savage Spanish behavior and consistently noble Indian resistance, de Soto dies in 1542 of fever and is buried in the great river he discovered. He is buried in stealth, because he had represented himself to the Indians as immortal.

At first glance, this story involving Renaissance Spaniards and Stone Age Indians appears to have nothing to do with the American South and with Lytle's relationship to his region. Although the wilderness de Soto wanders later became a big portion of the Confederacy, no one would want to claim that in subject and setting the novel deals in any usual sense with "the matter of the South." So why, after a biography, a symposium, and a novel, all thoroughly southern in subject and setting, did Lytle choose this story? In meaning, the novel is most decidedly an outgrowth of its author's southern sensibility, a literary flowering of Lytle's Agrarian thinking.

Lytle has spoken of the risk historical fiction should take "of forcing from a fragment of history its intrinsic meaning," and he seems fully to have decided upon the intrinsic meaning of de Soto's Florida expedition even in the earliest planning stages of the novel. In a January, 1938, letter to his Bobbs-Merrill editor, D. L. Chambers, Lytle speaks of writing a "series of novels which would be progressive in time" and in which "the new world will be seen as the old world's sin, even its destruction." Lytle continues, "After looking over the field very carefully, I've settled on De Soto's entry into the country in 1539 as the proper subject for the first novel." Then, after giving a rough précis of the projected book's plot, Lytle says the following about its intrinsic meaning: "Under the influence of gold, that is the materialistic view of the world, the mind of Christendom, and its spirit, sets out on its dance of death. The small army will have all the forms of its chivalry, but it is not seeking to deliver the Holy Sepulchre from the hands of the infidels. It is seeking the essence of materialism, its own spiritual destruction." [2]

The letter is a remarkable encapsulation of the thematic burden of the novel that was completed three years later. The theme can best be seen in the spiritual suicide of the book's two main characters, de Soto and his subordinate Nuno de Tovar. Lytle wrote in another letter: "They find no gold, but in their search for it the two men, de Soto and Tovar, each the obverse of the other, accept the world and become protestant or unchristian. De Soto by will, Tovar by the senses, the two men who always accept the world. In the progress of the drama, de Soto loses everything but will, Tovar everything but the attention to his senses." [3]

Sensuality is the instrument of Tovar's spiritual suicide. Second in command at the outset of the expedition and also the story's main narrator, Tovar is soon broken to the ranks because of an illicit affair with young Leonora de Bobadilla, de Soto's ward. At the fateful assignation, Tovar looks up from a hammock of vines through the mist-shrouded trees of the Cuban wilderness and muses, "We might be together at the middle of the world." Leonora whispers, "Not even the celebrated Court of Angels can see us here" (91). Tovar is unaware of the full meaning of his words. The erotic tumult in his heart is leading him ever farther away from Christian renunciation of worldliness. As for Leonora's words, the story makes clear they are wrong, though there is a quality about the New World that invites prelapsarian dreams of moral impunity—dreams that inevitably canker. Is the bloom of the New World garden meretricious? Morally neutral, the New World garden most frequently reflects the state of mind of its would-be interpreter. In pleasant circumstances, a buoyant and forgetful Tovar can think of this teeming wilderness as "a land for ease and riches and pleasure," where "love was still innocent" (303). But immediately after the catastrophe of Leonora's dis-

2. Andrew Lytle, Foreword to *Alchemy* (Winston-Salem, 1979), vi; Lytle to D. L. Chambers, January 27, 1938, quoted in Noel Polk, "Andrew Nelson Lytle: A Bibliography of His Writings," *Mississippi Quarterly,* XXIII (1970), 453–55.

3. Lytle to Chambers, n.d., quoted in *ibid,* 456.

covered pregnancy and his demotion, the wilderness seems to be something else, for Tovar projects his own dark carnality, his heart of darkness, into it. Wandering dazedly into the pioneer sanctuary, Tovar sees vegetation curling through a chink behind the crucifix and cries hysterically, "The sap, Father! In God's house" (92). The primal sap, though, is the sap of his own libido.

Later, when the expedition reaches paradisal Cutifichiqui, Tovar sinks even deeper into the trammels of the world. After a weary series of disappointing Indian towns, Cutifichiqui is as attractive as its pearl-bedecked chieftainess, and the beguiling custom here is to value an unmarried girl in rising proportion to the number of lovers she has had. The Indian queen tells de Soto his men are free to woo, and Tovar, who desires the queen's waiting woman, soon wins his leman in the hills outside the town. Shortly before encountering Tsianina, though, Tovar chances upon an ominous symbol of Cutifichiqui's ultimate meaning for the invading Christians, especially himself. He hears a flapping and a cry in the cedars, then comes upon a hawk and snake fighting, the hawk entangled in the snake's coils (304). There is an analogy between the "bird of princes" that Tovar beholds in distress and the conquistadors, for the Christian soldiers of Charles V's Holy Roman Empire are, in bewitching Cutifichiqui, risking the coils of earthbound heathenism, or spiritual death.

The symbol of the hawk and snake, however, is not admonition enough. Tovar quickly comes to see Cutifichiqui as "one long idyll" in which, as in a dream, "those desires impossible to the awakened senses are gratified," and he wants to settle there (306). When de Soto sets in motion the army's impending departure—plundering the Indian temple, taking the queen hostage—Tovar reacts in symbolic protest by marrying Tsianina Indian fashion. Observing pagan ritual, he walks through the night past the scalp poles and enters the dark lodge. Feeling a mixture of nausea and desire, he slips into the animal skins with his bride to couple in the presence of her kin. What before "had seemed so simple and innocent" is tonight "only feeling and darkness, feeling in darkness, pure and sharp, disembodied as a flame, drawing and consuming the flesh like dry dead wood until of itself it went out, spent by its own fury" (322). Afterward, the bigamous man of sensation understands only too well that, "following de Soto, the Christians had stumbled upon the world and before any knew it, all were drawn fast by its coils" (324).

Lust is not the only thing that draws Tovar to the "body of the world" and makes him a man of the senses (324). A further level of his spiritual decay is the hollowness of his nominally Christian chivalry. (As Lytle said to Chambers, "The small army will have all the forms of its chivalry, but it is not seeking to deliver the Holy Sepulchre from the hands of the infidels.") Tovar exults in his fighting skill as a Christian warrior, but in La Florida the old symbolism of Christian militance begins to lose its legitimacy. This becomes clear amidst the carnage of Mauvilla as Tovar toys with an Indian adversary, pricking him lightly with his lance and cruelly delaying the fatal stroke. Glorying egotistically in his sense of power, "godlike in its aloofness," Tovar is no self-renouncing, death-courting Christian warrior, but just a warrior (356).[4] When the weaponless Indian hurls himself into a burning lodge, there silently gazing out as he blisters and dies, Tovar is humbled by this "superior act of manhood" (356). Tovar's late-flung lance leans in the flames, where having been bisected by an arrow, it forms a cross that burns impotently. Is it the cross of salvation these gold seekers have brought to the New World? The irony is clear. The Indian proves himself superior both in manhood and in self-abnegation, the latter making him, in a figurative sense, a better "Christian." As Tovar thinks later, obsessed by this incident, "Could a mere heathen so mortify his flesh, lacking the example of Lord Christ to sustain him, while he, a Christian, must have showed his feather?" (361–62).

As for Tovar's commander, the instrument of de Soto's spiritual suicide is not sensuality but pride. The supreme example of it is also the central symbolic action of the book, the confrontation at mass between de Soto and Father Francisco after the Mauvilla

4. On Tovar's fleshly "self-deification," see Robert G. Benson, "Yankees of the Race: The Decline and Fall of Hernando de Soto," in Bradford (ed.), *The Form Discovered,* 94.

disaster. The wheat and molds having burned at Mauvilla, along
with the Cutifichiquian pearls, this mass is the last at which the
Host will be lifted above the altar, then consumed. The mass proceeds, all the army present, "and then it happened. When Father
Francisco had reached the place in the service where he was
about to eat God's body . . . he turned toward the people with
the holy Host in his hand, holding it upright above the paten"
(367). He calls out, "Hernando de Soto, come before me" (367).
With de Soto kneeling before the altar, the priest raises the Host
over the Adelantado's head. "By this God, whom I hold here
in my hands, I warn, I beseech, I command that you now do
that which you have not wished to do, which in your stubborn
avarice and pride you have refused—Go out of this land!" (368).
It is not in de Soto to curb his Promethean drive, though, and
finally he will only say, "I believe it is God's will that this land be
pacified. Pacified it shall be. There is your answer" (373).

Tovar, one of the communicants watching this mass in sus-
pense, interprets the situation with a wisdom beyond his ability
to perform: "He [de Soto] had set his private will outside the
guidance and discipline of the Church, the will which, unrestrained, serves only the senses, as the senses only the flesh. He, a
layman, had undertaken to interpret God's mind. This is what his
decision meant, no matter if he denied or disguised it. From here
it is only one step further to supplant God's will by man's and call
it divine—man made God, man with all his frailties and pride setting up the goods of the world over the good of heavenly grace"
(374). Turning his back on the altar and facing the wilderness,
Tovar wonders, "Where would it lead them all?" (374). The answer is to probable physical death and certain spiritual death.
Significantly, the men stop going to confession after the Mauvilla
mass, and on Sabbath days, with "no blood or body to lift to the
altar, the congregation sullenly and unreasonably connected
the absence of God's body with the Governor's defiance" (382).
The men feel somehow relieved of personal spiritual responsibility, now reposing that responsibility in de Soto, the man of unchristian will. This turn of events vividly represents, in the terms

of Lytle's letter to Chambers, "the mind of Christendom . . . on its dance of death."

Details of de Soto's character that were revealed earlier show their significance in the light of his impious assertion of private will at the Mauvilla mass. In retrospect, the aloofness and hatred of dependence of Hernando the young page prefigure the supplanting of God's will by de Soto the man (21–23). Similarly, Tovar's first glimpse of de Soto, when Tovar is dying of fever in Panama, is of eyes that "rather looked in than out and looked not to see but to devour" (20). Tovar remembers, "Perhaps it was my own fevered vision, but they seemed to be sinking into his flesh, towards that dark interior where lay the only sustenance able to glut their hunger." (20). That sustenance is Promethean pride. And, as the captain of conquistadors, de Soto can give free rein to that pride. "What prince in all the known world," he exults to his wife, Ysabella, "commands such desperate measures, such unfailing obedience?" (66). Ysabella herself experiences a portion of the brutal energy behind de Soto's words when virtually raped by him before the departure from Spain (67–68). Later, the violence that is a by-product of his monomaniacal will shows itself repeatedly in the wilderness. The casual air with which he watches an Indian patriot thrown to the dogs is an example (158–61).

Perhaps the most significant portent of de Soto's blasphemy at Mauvilla is the feast of the mulberry moon at Cutifichiqui, the occasion of the first open clash between de Soto and Father Francisco. The priest calls the celebration a "feast of death," forbids attendance, and warns that the Indian rites are made "to the moon. To the pagan goddess of the woods and fields and streams. To her these lost and deluded souls make sacrifice. I call on you, Hernando de Soto, to take no part in it" (299). De Soto shrugs off the priest's apprehensions, explaining attendance as a matter of diplomacy. Symbolically, however, the army's presence at the evening's moon-worship—especially de Soto's presence—is more than mere diplomacy, as the climactic rejection of Church authority at Mauvilla confirms. In the course of their hunt for gold, the conquistadors become lodgers "at the moon's inn," a Spanish term for "sleeping outside," which, as Robert Benson has pointed out, comes to mean "life in the world," that is, unchristian life in the temporal world.[5]

In view of the moon motif in the novel, it is significant that over the predawn Mauvilla mass the moon presides "as thin as a wafer"; for with de Soto's blasphemy, the thin wafer of the false moon replaces the communion wafer in the life of the army and its commander (369). De Soto's figurative devotion to the moon lies ultimately in his perverse willfulness, which, as Lytle observed, forces him "to deny the Host and become his private interpreter of God."[6] In its last two years of grim wandering, the army becomes wholly the reflection of this monstrous will. "So long as the Governor's will maintained its pure, direct drive," thinks Tovar, "so long as it followed avidly the promise of the world, followed it without weakening or allowing the golden image which drew it on to tarnish, that long and no longer would the expedition hold together and thrive" (384). Only at the expedition's disastrous end—the army lost, and reduced to posturing and child killing in its dealings with the Indians—does the Adelantado realize that the corrupt will of the self-exalting materialist is insufficient.

It is, however, only de Soto's ghost—or what the overwrought Tovar thinks is his ghost—that realizes the inadequacy of the corrupt will. Hurrying back to his ailing commander from a terrorist strike against the Nilco, Tovar rushes into de Soto's lodge and at first sees nothing. Then a supine figure in furbished armor from spur to casque materializes out of the moonlight: an apparition of de Soto. From the shining casque issues a voice. The New World, says de Soto's ghost, "is the Moon's Inn for all, heathen and Christian alike. It can never be more than a temporary abode, a stopping place of the variable seasons, where the moon is host and the reckoning counted up in sweat, in hunger, and in blood." The voice continues: "The will is not enough. It is not

5. *Ibid.*

6. Lytle to Chambers, n.d., quoted in Polk, "Andrew Nelson Lytle: A Bibliography," 456.

enough for one bent on his own destruction. Did I lead the chivalry of Spain to the sacred groves, the blessed land of Jerusalem? No, I am the alchemical captain, the adventurer in gold" (397). The "alchemical captain" journeys not to the "sacred groves" but to the moon's inn and, in the language of Lytle's letter quoted earlier, finds "the essence of materialism"—his "own spiritual destruction."

Both de Soto and Tovar, in terms of the book's symbolism, become moonstruck. In a letter explaining "how the title fits very well," Lytle remarks that "it needs another word before it"; that is, the book's meaning implies a word to be filled in mentally before the phrase *At the Moon's Inn.*[7] In view of the theme of spiritual suicide, that word would be *Death: Death at the Moon's Inn.* The closing words of de Soto's ghost are suggestive in this regard. Murmuring that "the universal menstruum [fabled solvent of alchemical lore] is this," he stretches forth into the moonlight a skeletal hand—the hand of death (398). For all who join the alchemist's soul-corrupting search for gold, death is the only universal solvent.

When Tovar finds de Soto's burial detachment on the banks of the Mississippi, the men shudder as they stare into the hurrying current of the Adelantado's watery grave. Someone says, "It is the turning of the tide" (400). Thus, even as a corpse, de Soto proves the creature of the tide-governing moon.

Given the novel's concern with materialism and spiritual self-destruction, its connection with the modern time and southern place of its origin is clear. Materialism and spiritual self-destruction are precisely the modern-age evils Lytle had decried in the 1930s, in "The Hind Tit," "The Backwoods Progression," "The Small Farm Secures the State," and the other Agrarian essays. Whereas gold is the symbol of ruinous materialism in the de Soto novel, the Yankee ledger, for instance, is that symbol in the essay Lytle wrote for *I'll Take My Stand.* Thus, in *At the Moon's Inn,* despite the chronological remove of its setting, the action reveals meanings consistent with the passionate ideas that had

7. *Ibid.*

earlier grown directly out of Lytle's experience as a southerner.

One of the reasons Lytle wrote to Chambers that, "after look-ing over the field very carefully," he had "settled on De Soto's entry into the country" as his subject is that he saw de Soto as the prototypal modern. In "The Backwoods Progression," Lytle had described the self-deifying mentality of modernism thus: "Man begins to think he is a god, but he has only unshackled his will. A curious, modern Prometheus, he has stolen no living but an abstract fire."[8] This could be a description of Lytle's de Soto, for it is similar to Tovar's assessment of de Soto's unrestrained willfulness: "From here it is only one step further to supplant God's will by man's and call it divine—man made God, man with all his frailties and pride setting up the goods of the world over the good of heavenly grace" (374).

De Soto, as Robert Benson says, is an "Overreacher," the kins-man of Prometheus, Faustus, and Lucifer. The grasping modern whom Lytle pilloried in his Agrarian excursions of the 1930s has the same kinsmen. The dangerous modern position, Lytle wrote in "The Backwoods Progression," is that the state "exists for the private will. It then follows that any individual who is cunning enough, or powerful enough, or lucky enough, may make of the State . . . or even of the world, a possession answerable to the commands of his desire." This form of Promethean overreaching, or in Lytle's words, "the old war against the gods," is apparent in de Soto's aspiration to possess the New World.[9]

The irreligion and presumption that accompany de Soto's overreaching are characteristically modern evils in southern Agrarian eyes. In "The Hind Tit," for instance, Lytle had given the call to reject the irreligious power worship inherent in the mod-ern infatuation with science (a power worship that can be seen as another "moonstruck" form of materialistically accepting "the world"). "Seek a priesthood that may manifest the will and intel-ligence to renounce science and search out the Word in the au-thorities," the Agrarian Lytle had polemicized. Of the modern

8. Lytle, "The Backwoods Progression," 428–29.
9. Benson, "Yankees of the Race," in Bradford (ed.), *The Form Discovered,* 85; Lytle, "The Backwoods Progression," 413.

evil of presumption, he had written in "The Small Farm Secures the State" that "when religion grows formless and weak, it is because man in his right role as the protagonist in the great conflict is forgotten or disbelieved. He becomes vainglorious and thinks he may conquer nature." In contrast to the archetypically vainglorious de Soto, the Agrarian knows that nature may be *used* but never, without penalty, violently subverted entirely to man's will.[10]

In an indirect, wholly undoctrinal way, *At the Moon's Inn* puts the religious humanism of Agrarianism within the context of Western, not just American, history. In a direct, tractarian way, the seminal essay "The Backwoods Progression" had done the same thing, linking Lytle's southern loyalties to the model of order he perceived in the High Middle Ages. A character in *At the Moon's Inn*—the old marshal of Seville at de Soto's predeparture promotional feast—represents precisely this ideal. This battle-scarred hidalgo had been among the knights who had driven the Moors out of Spain forty-five years earlier, and he now thinks the prospective New World adventurers should instead break lances for Christ against the Moors in Africa or against Soliman's Janizaries in Constantinople. Specifically, he is suspicious of the adventurers' infatuation with the riches of the New World. "Shall we let perish our immortal souls," he asks, "for a policy like unto that of the Venetian state which pays tribute to Soliman that courtesans may have spices in their meats?" (46). Thinking aloud, he continues:

> Granada fell in 1492. Later that year Columbus made such a hole in Christendom I fear me it can never be plugged. I had seen the adventurer about Their Majesties' pavilions earlier in the siege. I had thought him an alchemist. I knew he was no soldier. And, for truth, he did turn out a kind of alchemy, for too much gold pours into this frugal land. Remember this, young captains. On that blessed day when Dona Ysabel rode in triumph into Granada, she held in her hands the sceptre of Castile. It was a slight thing of silver gilt. Yet it

10. Lytle, "The Hind Tit," in *I'll Take My Stand*, 244, and "The Small Farm Secures the State," in *Who Owns America?* 247–48.

had brought low the Infidels who had usurped our kingdoms for seven hundred years. (47)

Then he lifts his cup, alone, to "that poverty of the Cross which is Spain!" (47).

The old marshal speaks from the moral center of the novel, and he proves right on every score. Under the influence of materialism, the young captains, certainly Tovar and de Soto, let perish their immortal souls; the symbolism of Christian militance—breaking lances for Christ and the "poverty of the Cross"—becomes a sham in La Florida; and alchemical Columbus, his influence registering in de Soto, seems indeed to have made a nearly unpluggable hole in Christendom.[11]

Five years before Lytle began to work on *At the Moon's Inn,* back in the days of heated Agrarian campaigning, "The Backwoods Progression" had broadened the scope of his southern allegiances by presenting the Old South as a New World reflection of an older Christian inheritance, a throwback to some of the better features of the premodern, medieval world. If Lytle cut his image of both the southern past and the European past to the pattern of his heart's desire, he did so in passionate defense of his region's demonstrable difference from the aggressive nation as a whole. Lytle's implicit sympathy with the old marshal and what he stands for did not grow impersonally and dispassionately from a study of history books, but from the turbulent, personal experience of being a southerner; its ultimate source lay in Lytle's desire as a southerner in the midst of wrenching change to cling to certain traditional values. Thus in the background behind the marshal is Lytle's southern *pietas:* his reverence for the things of the spirit, for communal attachment to place, and for traditional ideals of honorable human behavior.

At the Moon's Inn dramatizes a tension between antithetical world views—one secular, the other religious—and this tension had concerned Lytle as early as the 1925 Scopes trial, when

11. See M. E. Bradford, "Toward a Dark Shape: Lytle's 'Alchemy' and the Conquest of the New World," in Bradford (ed.), *The Form Discovered,* 60.

northern vehemence had seemed to the young Tennessean to reflect "belief in a secular instead of a divine order of the universe."[12] Lytle's southern instincts helped shape the meaning of
At the Moon's Inn; there is a fundamental affinity between Agrarian convictions and the novel's moral dimension. Agrarianism
is a philosophy for interpreting life that involves a chastening
awareness of human limitations and a reverent regard for the
community, for nature, and for God. In de Soto, Lytle located the
epitome of the Faustian side of North American history, for de
Soto violates all of the Agrarian sentiments; he elevates his will to
godlike proportions, isolates himself from his fellow men, bru-
talizes nature, and defies spiritual authority. Despite initial appearances, *At the Moon's Inn* has deep roots in that place that
Lytle called the American backwoods—that base of operations
against a moonstruck America, the South.

12. Lytle, "They Took Their Stand," 116.

VII

The Dialectical Imagination and
A Name for Evil

Whether the past can be reclaimed by an act of will is one of the questions Lytle's third novel confronts, and in doing so, it brings scorching ironies to bear against modernism, as did *At the Moon's Inn.* However, *A Name for Evil,* published in 1947, is also an unflinching look at the ambiguities of a southern allegiance that craves the past. It is a deeply ironic circumstance that the protagonist of the novel is something of a philosopher of traditionalism, for the story's subtleties, especially its doubling motif, demonstrate that he is in reality an enemy of tradition. Thus *A Name for Evil* is a striking example of the simultaneous objectivity and engagement of Lytle's artistic sensibility. The South fuels his imagination without compromising it in the course of this dialectical quarrel with the self.

Set on a Tennessee farm during one year of World War II, *A Name for Evil* is, at least on the surface, a ghost story involving the malevolent shade of a long-dead former owner, and a husband and wife who have come to restore the property. The shade is that of old Major Brent, a ruthless man who, at the end of his life in the late 1860s, had done a strange thing. After bringing The Grove to perfection—the formal garden a masterpiece, the grain and tobacco fields at maximum yield—the Major dispossessed his inheritors. His face shining, he announced that the land had achieved its ultimate crop and would never be tilled again. Then he gave his sons one thousand dollars each, sent them off the land, and deeded the estate to his spinster daughter.

Seventy-five years later, a collateral descendant of the Major buys The Grove in hopes of restoring it to beauty and abundance. This man, Henry Brent, has taken on a formidable task, for the farm has suffered in the hands of absentee landlords and shiftless tenants. The soil has been abused, brambles have overtaken the fields, and years of "poor-white grime" have sunk into the decaying house. The most formidable part of the task, though, is coping with the presence of the old Major. He recurrently appears to Henry—gazing insolently from the gallery, peering malevolently into the study, fumbling at the bedroom doorknob, materializing on the bank of a sinkhole—until the tragic conclusion. The Major, Henry becomes convinced, has designs against Ellen, Henry's wife. Planning to remove to town at least until their child is born, Henry and his pregnant wife are delayed by a winter storm. When the wintry weather finally breaks in a morning of thick fog, they go into the formal garden to enjoy the preternatural whiteness. They become disoriented in the fog, though, and Henry leaves Ellen to search for the gate. When in panic he returns to Ellen, she backs onto the platform of the rotten springhouse, the planks give way, and in the arms of Major Brent she falls to her death.

That is the outline of the ghost-story surface of the novel. *A Name for Evil,* however, is not simply a ghost story but also a complex psychological study in which the ghostly Major Brent represents the shadow self of the obsessed narrator, Henry Brent.[1] In other words, Henry Brent—the only person to "see" the Major during the nine months of the action—is a paranoiac haunted not by a putatively real ghost but by a projected side of himself. Since the book is entirely dramatic, the narrative's guides

---

1. Charles C. Clark mentions the story's *"Doppelganger* effect" in "*A Name for Evil:* A Search for Order," in Bradford (ed.), *The Form Discovered,* 26.

to interpretation are necessarily subtle, residing entirely in the largely unwitting self-revelations of a madman as he broods retrospectively over his tragedy.

As he follows the methodical backtracking of the first-person narration, the reader frequently encounters parallel images of the Major and Henry Brent. First, there is Henry's initial twilight sighting, from a distance, of a figure on the upper gallery, who disappears in the direction of Henry's study (which had formerly been the Major's room). When Henry bumps into his wife immediately afterward, she alarmedly remarks that he looks "like a ghost," an analogy that seems inconsequential at this point but accrues significance as the doubling motif is evoked further.[2] It is strange that Henry rushes into the house with no thought of picking up a weapon against a marauder and that, finding no one inside, he says that nothing is just what he knew he would find (195). Does Henry sense that the "anonymous regions" into which the intruder disappears are the anonymous regions of his own psyche (196)?

A particularly striking example of doubling occurs when Henry confronts the Major at the study window. "There at the very top of the window, just out from the edge of one of the blinds which had blown to, I saw a face. It pressed against the pane in passionate anguish, its nose crushed white and its eyes, as limpid as a hawk's and dark as sin, leveled upon mine." Even in memory, says Henry, "it comes back in *the intimacy I was made to feel with him.* When his glance left mine to travel over the room, I was ignored as if I did not exist, or *as if I were so deep in his purpose as to be his other self*" (203, italics mine). From this experience, Henry drew the knowledge that he himself was the key to what the Major sought, "the door through which he [the Major] must pass to his loathsome desire" (204). The secret-sharer motif suggested in these lines is underscored by the fact that Henry goes

2. Andrew Lytle, *A Name for Evil* (New York, 1947). The novel is more readily accessible in the volume *A Novel, a Novella and Four Stories,* quotation above from 195. All page references are to this collection and hereinafter cited parenthetically in the text.

out to the stairway and duplicates the vanished figure's position at the study window. He peers around the blind, just as he had seen the Major do, and at this moment his black tenant, Johnny, walks into the study, sees the staring face, and turns in fright. This is an early indication of what becomes increasingly clear: Henry Brent gives the shadowy Major "the substance he lacks" and is himself the chief horror at The Grove (210).

In another example of double imagery, the Major appears one night at the door to the room where Ellen lies sleeping. Henry, who has been working late, approaches his "guest" (a suggestive term) and feels suspended with him "in some intermediate world" (222). The phantom disappears, but Henry is now convinced that the Major intends violence, perhaps sexual, against Ellen. Then, mirroring the Major's recent visitation, Henry stands at Ellen's bedroom door, his hand on the knob. He enters and, in a rush of sexual desire, rips his shirt in his haste to lie with her. Waking late the next morning, he finds Ellen in the garden, whose ruin she has secretly been repairing for weeks. He sneaks up behind her and, silently watching her weed a pathway, admires the lines of her neck "with the sweet sense of possession." She has the innocent air, he muses, of "the sacrificial victim" (229). Her labor, however, seems too rapid, too tense; it is "as though she felt behind her the shadow of the taskmaster" (229). Henry thinks that taskmaster is the Major, but the reader may wonder otherwise. Not only does Henry hover behind Ellen in as sinister fashion as he imagines the Major might, but having come to loathe the restoration project, he has gradually left the tasks of regeneration to her (see, for instance, 250–51).

In light of these and other instances of doubling, the crucial question concerns the meaning of the implied parallel between Henry Brent and the Major. More specifically, what is it in Henry that links him to the old eccentric who dispossessed his posterity in a gesture of monstrous egotism?

Henry Brent possesses a great deal of egotism, eerily akin to the Major's. For instance, he soon mentally reduces his attempted restoration of The Grove to an absurdly competitive war of egos with his long-dead relative. "Was he really a better man than I?" Henry frets (191). He cannot stand the thought of being surpassed by anyone, not even by a dead man from a former era, and he often thinks of his predecessor with envy and hatred, even before the spectral visitations begin. The Grove, Henry complains, was the Major's conception. "It bore the stamp of his mind and his will. And his mind and his will *I* was restoring and the better I did it the more I submerged my personality and the greener his kept" (191). Like the Major, who in "vanity and by will" had refused to submerge his ego in the continuity of the family on the land, Henry is not one to submerge his imperious sense of self in anything, despite his occasional rhetoric to the contrary (266).

Perhaps the most shocking indication of Henry's egomaniacal willfulness is his effectual rape of Ellen one night. It is at the onset of winter as the action draws toward its catastrophic close.[3] Henry is convinced that the Major's "ghostly purpose had advanced almost to the moment of resolution," and in his growing insanity, he is further convinced that Ellen is somehow implicated in the Major's machinations (267). He has not told her yet about his several confrontations with Major Brent's ghost, but by now he is sure she knows the Major all too well. His dark imaginings have sexual undertones, for he suspects in her a desire "to try the multiplicity of those dark practices his ghostly whisper set her longing for" (283). It is a measure of his perversion that the thought of sexual evil in her excites his own evil desires, for he sees in Ellen "that fusion of innocence and desire which makes ecstatic the eye of the sinner as he ravishes and cleans himself upon what his glance devours" (270). This "sinner" he

3. Concerning the archetypal level of the story, Lytle writes the following to Douglas Jarrold, July 9, 1947, in Lytle Papers: "The underlying myth of which the book is the symbol is the Thammuz or Adonis myth. To avoid allegory I tried to dissolve the myth in action which would represent it, so that if the reader is so minded he can recreate the symbol out of the action. . . . Neither the symbol nor the myth is private. My only tampering with it is to introduce it into a world where it fails. Under the protestant will there is no regeneration, the sacrifice does not inseminate; hence there is no spring."

believes to be the Major, but it is Henry himself. The ravishing and cleaning are Henry's own.

Imagining that Ellen's sleepy eyes focus "on some reverie of phantoms . . . she now met with urgent, feverish need," Henry enters the bedroom and begins a conversation full of dark innuendos on his part and innocent replies on Ellen's (267). When she mentions his neglect of her, he asks insinuatingly, "But does it matter so much to you?" Ellen decides to reveal her presentiment that she is pregnant. "Yes, it has mattered," she replies. "but it may not any more. There may be someone to take your place" (269). These innocent words confirm Henry's suspicion that the Major grows in Ellen's desire "like a cancer" and is about to take his place (270).

> I was the one from whose arms she had been snatched by lot, and as I stood there, for a moment helpless, all my old longing for her love, the keener for the sense of the loss I would suffer, took hold of me. "No love shall supplant our love," I whispered, advancing.
> "No, no," she said, drawing back. "Don't ruin everything."
> But I did not hear. My hand pressed on the hot circle the lamp chimney made. The light flickered and then went out. For an instant the tongue of flame leaped at my flesh. My mouth swam in hot jets of pain and the silence swelled into one great swoon. She for a little resisted my arms, but at last I plunged into darkness. (271)

Before this night, Henry had believed the Major on the verge of loosing his "last onset" (267). Henry has proved to be the agent of that onset. De Soto's rape of Ysabella in *At the Moon's Inn* demonstrates the same blind will and monstrous self-absorption.

This egotism that Henry shares with his double is largely what prevents him from being the traditional man he professes to be. Truly to possess a traditional sensibility is to discipline the raw ego within inherited patterns of conduct—ritual, manners, and institutions, especially the institution of the family. As Lytle once stated, the traditional man has "location, which means property, which means the family and the communion of families which is the state. Otherwise, as now, the individual is at the mercy of his ego."[4] In his last worldly act, the Major had chosen deliberately to violate the canons of tradition and elevate his own ego to god-like preeminence. Henry is less consciously at the mercy of his ego, but his egotism is equally a violation of tradition and is equally destructive. Thus he speaks unwitting truth when he asks, concerning his probe into the Major's tradition-affronting history, "Where will it bring me . . . this cold scent, but where all false trails lead—back upon myself?" (238). Akin to the Major's dispersion of his heirs, for instance, is Henry's professed apathy toward having children at all (see 216–17). And analogous to the Major's burial of six worn-out women in the garden (all but one having died, according to their tombstones, "in childbed") is Henry's culpability for the death of his own pregnant wife in the same garden. On the surface, Henry acknowledges and seems to honor the belief that, as he says, "woman is the carrier of tradition" (244). But in his subterranean recoil from tradition and the checks it would place on his ego, he ultimately scares Ellen into her grave.

The final scene takes place in the fog-shrouded garden after three weeks of snowbound isolation. During these weeks, Ellen has waited on Henry attentively, watching him nervously. One can discern through the screen of his narration her desperate hope that their imminent removal to town will mend him. With his late-night wandering, the rape, and, finally, his mad talk about the haunting of The Grove ("Your eyes. Your eyes," Ellen cries), Henry has brought his wife to near hysteria. So, as they walk in the fog, Ellen is understandably panicky when, near the spring-house, they lose sight of the garden gate. Henry leaves Ellen, searches through the "white blindness," and then, suddenly filled with dread, loses his way back to her. Silently, he walks in circles, even his sense of time disordered, until he finds himself once again near Ellen.

> There she was, barely visible in the opaque light, directly in front of me. She had not heard me come up. She stood with her head

4. Andrew Lytle, "How Many Miles to Babylon?" in Rubin and Jacobs (eds.), *Southern Renascence,* 33.

slightly bent, in the frozen tension of one who looks down into an abyss. Her hands were clasped over her bosom. I felt a boundless relief, but as I looked more sharply I saw that she was listening to no spoken words, but to some secret communication she was well practiced in deciphering. The whole appalling truth was before me.

"Ellen!" I screamed.

My anguish and the fixity of my purpose to save her gave to my cry its unearthly quality. She bounded forward, whirled around and, looking blindly at me, made the sound of a wounded beast. And then she saw me. For one instant she turned upon me a wild, transforming stare, when she began to back slowly away, moaning, "No, no, no," over and over again. (326)

As she backs toward the springhouse, Henry sees behind her the waiting figure of the Major. When the rotten platform splinters under Ellen, Henry rushes down the trapdoor steps, only to find a corpse. "Already I knew what it was I held in my arms, and I knew that at last Major Brent had triumphed and I was alone" (327).

The part of Henry that is Major Brent—the solipsistic, tradition-blighting ego—has triumphed indeed. The wild fright that brings Ellen to her death has nothing to do with a demon lover; it is the fright of witnessing Henry's affliction.[5] She runs not to any discarnate Major Brent but away from Henry as he gapes in the throes of his hallucination. Having killed his wife and the unborn heir in her womb, Henry, just like the Major, has "abandoned *The Grove* to sterility, to a withering up of the traditional vine" (243). Thus the imagined ghoul on the platform, whose "hateful features" Henry "had come to know as well as . . . [his] own," is Henry himself (326).

The circumstances of Lytle's life during the composition of *A Name for Evil,* from 1943 to 1947, are relevant to the story's concern with tradition and the ways its restoration can go awry. Not long after the publication of *At the Moon's Inn,* Lytle decided to restore an old house and make a go of farming on land

---

5. For commentary on the story's relationship to *The Turn of the Screw,* see Jack De Bellis, "Andrew Lytle's *A Name for Evil,*" *Critique,* VIII (Spring, 1966), 26–40.

he had bought north of Nashville, near Portland, Tennessee. (He named the farm Cornsilk after the old family property in north Alabama.) Thus, while wrestling with the difficulties of regeneration, he wrote a book concerning, among other things, the difficulties of regeneration. That Lytle knew intimately the particulars of house restoration and Tennessee farm life—how wallpaper is steamed, how tobacco is fired—helps account for the utter verisimilitude of the novel's setting. And though the transaction between life and art need not be autobiographical, and usually is not, this novel seems obliquely to represent an interesting adjustment in Lytle's Agrarianism, a further stage in the evolution of his thoughts about the traditional life.

Of his Portland farm, Lytle writes:

> It had been a good farm with a racetrack and a smokehouse which held a hundred hogs. There were three tobacco barns, a hog barn, an inadequate stock barn, two tenant houses, a schoolhouse (in which I raised turkeys), and the usual Tennessee country house, built of yellow poplar. It was sound but looked bad, as tenants had lived in it for thirty years. The blinds to the windows had been taken off to make hogpens. There were no fences. The cistern was out of use. The tenants were farming it in patches and letting briars and sprouts take over large parts of the fields. It was called "a throwed-away farm."[6]

Its former vitality gone, the Portland farm's general similarity to The Grove is readily recognizable.

Further, many of Lytle's letters from this period contain comments concerning his own state of mind that to some degree make one think of Henry Brent. Assuredly, the restoration process at Lytle's farm had its pleasures, but its ordeals are the recurrent theme in his letters. For instance, to Allen Tate, he writes:

> I've had no chance to finish the story [A Name for Evil was initially projected as a short story]. If we can get our own apartment ready to live in and let the rest of the house go for the time being, I will be able to get down to work again. It is tiring to be thwarted in these material matters, like one of those dreams of running in mo-

6. Lytle, *A Wake for the Living,* 262.

lasses with a monster after you. . . . Hard as this winter promises to be, I think we will stick it out here and give this place a thorough trial, although I have had so much trouble with it, at times I've grown to dislike it.[7]

With this confession of bouts of aversion one might compare Henry Brent's remark after two seasons on his farm: "I was beginning to loathe everything about *The Grove,* for the place had become the symbol of the waste of our lives, the subversion of my one idea" (251).

In another letter to Tate, after a winter of being "mud and ice bound," Lytle writes:

> I am making a heroic effort to get this place in a material way pretty well established this year; so that I can cut loose from it [that is, be free to write]. . . . I've done a good deal, but there is much to do yet. Lon [Brainard Cheney] got us the lights, I got a new road cut, et cetera, but none of these matters are completed entirely. . . . At times I do not see my way clear, but if I am right, this place will beat for me universities, hack work. The times are difficult anyway, but I have hardened myself to the responsibility of my present condition. . . . It's a gamble, but I am too deeply in to pull out, even if I knew of another gamble that might seem propitious.
>
> I have learned much that will be of use. For example that regeneration is far more difficult than generation.

That fall, the difficulties of regeneration are still on his mind. It "has been a hard and frustrating year," he writes. The tobacco crop has been damaged; field hands are disappearing. "It is unpleasant to live in an unfinished house, where everything is inconvenient and the marks of thirty years of tenants confront you."[8] Henry Brent, too, speaks of "awakening to the real difficulties of regeneration" (248). Henry exclaims: "How blithely I had gone into this business! And truly the idea had seemed sound: establish my family in one location as a safeguard against the hazards of my uncertain profession [he is a novelist]; re-

7. Lytle to Tate, October 18, 1943, in Tate Papers.
8. Lytle to Tate, January 18, May 13, and October 16, 1944, in Tate Papers.

generate a family place and make up for the failure in trusteeship of those who had gone before" (182–83).

In accord with these perhaps surprising resemblances between Henry Brent and Lytle, Brent frequently talks extraordinarily like an Agrarian:

> *The Grove* at its heyday was a going concern in every way. No money was brought in from the outside to run it. The land maintained the economy of the house, its hospitality and gracious living. But since those days the country has become an extension of the town. Let us be frank. It is servile. Its mores, the price it gets for its products, the clothes it wears, almost what it thinks, are determined by an absentee master. You may name this master what you please. It matters little whether its elusive all-powerful mechanism is controlled by management or by labor. On either horn the farmer is gored. (190)

> This condition [the workman's lack of professional integrity] was not entirely the fault of those in public places; they were merely the representatives of this democracy of absolute corruption, for the evil had long been working in the yeast. Everywhere one felt a spiritual emasculation, for a man's final belief in himself comes from his attitude toward and his performance of his job. (248–49)

One hears in such pronouncements the echoes of Lytle's attacks in the 1930s on the economic and social confusion of modern society, and one sees the lineaments of his Agrarian defense, in "The Hind Tit," "The Backwoods Progression," and elsewhere, of a society of ceremony and role grounded in a concrete history.[9]

What Henry Brent says and what he does are seldom the same, though. As the doubling motif underscores, Henry is the creature, far more than he realizes, of the tradition-razing modernism he deplores. (Like Pleasant McIvor in *The Long Night*, Brent comes to personify what he professedly abhors.) Indeed, he is Lytle's representative of a "late world . . . where all is will." The Major's egomaniacal destruction of his posterity is a "foreshadowing," wrote Lytle to his editor in England, of the impious mod-

9. Other striking examples of Brent's "Agrarian" statements can be found on 171, 247, and 277.

ern's "assumption of godlike power." As Charles C. Clark has demonstrated, Henry Brent is incipiently a gnostic modern.[10] Henry even refers to himself as the "false romantic" who with "will and deliberation" hangs an obscuring veil between himself and "the true nature of reality." The false romantic, Henry continues, even begins to believe "the veil was hung by God, or in the most violent falsification of his nature, he becomes God" (182). Near the end of the novel, Henry briefly recognizes, with that flash of prescience of the mad, the destructive innocence of his motives at The Grove.

> False romantic that I was when I first came with my idea, how was I to know when I bought a run-down farm to restore that I had bought nothing, that the fiction to own, in spite of deed and possession, describes the most ephemeral of all artifices? How was I to know that I had put myself in way of the past and future, bemused by the mad fancy that I could reach into history and regenerate, a function proper only to a god? . . . In this fuller knowledge it came to me with the suddenness of revelation: was not my idea the obverse of Major Brent's act? (308)

Henry is right. His willful attempt to regenerate the past is the obverse of the Major's willful attempt to proscribe the future. It is somewhat surprising to find Lytle exploring the ambiguities of an attempted return to traditional ways after his arguing so zealously in the thirties for such a return. (The "answer," Lytle had earlier written, "lies in a return to a society where agriculture is practiced by most of the people.")[11] Why, after all, *cannot* Henry Brent "reach into history and regenerate"?

Interpretation of *A Name for Evil* and reflections on Lytle's personal experience intersect at this point, for Lytle discloses in this story a new stage in his thinking about the possibilities of the past—a new stage perhaps crystallized by his own experience with a "throwed-away farm." To wit, for the modern man to live in the country in hopes of isolatedly recovering a past way of life

10. Lytle to Tate, July 8, 1947, in Tate Papers; Lytle to Jarrold, July 9, 1947, in Lytle Papers; Clark, "*A Name for Evil:* A Search for Order," in Bradford (ed.), *The Form Discovered,* 26–29.
11. Lytle, "The Hind Tit," in *I'll Take My Stand,* 203.

is futile, given the fact that history, for better or worse, has utterly passed by that former way of life. This realization is implicit in the meaning of *A Name for Evil*. In 1930 Lytle suggested that a reconstitution of the still-vital shards of agrarian life was possible. In 1947 he suggests otherwise; the crucial moment has passed. Thus Henry Brent's attempt—or the attempt of any modern—to "reach into the past and regenerate" is indeed a waste of life. To pursue a way of life that can no longer be lived is to become at best a vestigial curiosity, at worst an overreacher swollen by will. Henry Brent is not merely a special case. Despite the singular horrors of his circumstance, his predicament as would-be restorer has a wider, emblematic significance.

A Name for Evil, then, reveals Lytle willing to concede that regenerating the rural, communal southern past is now impossible. In the 1940s, he sees farming as a way of life, indeed, the old order in general, as irretrievably moribund. The modern world may be a diminished world lacking community and communal values, but to deny it in an attempt to live as in the past is tantamount to setting up "the grave / In the house" (I am quoting from Tate's "Ode to the Confederate Dead," an interesting analogue). The modern southerner aware of his heritage may have "knowledge carried to the heart"; he may dimly understand "the vision" of an older South. But he nonetheless remains a watcher outside the graveyard wall, a modern partaking of the modern sensibility. Honor "the immoderate past" as he may, he remains cut off from it.[12] Indeed, the gravest irony of *A Name for Evil* is that the only connection with the past that Henry Brent is finally able to make is with Major Brent, the figurative harbinger of modernism.

This is hardly to say that the story constitutes a covert rejection of Agrarianism, though it does imply a change in Lytle's attitude toward what is programmatic in Agrarianism. It is not accurate to claim, as does John M. Bradbury, that "this novel seems the best single refutation of Agrarian-traditionalist positions that

12. Allen Tate, "Ode to the Confederate Dead," in *The Swimmers and Other Selected Poems* (New York, 1970), 17–19.

has been produced either by its enemies or its supporters."[13] The dynamic of the story suggests that the insoluble problem of history stands in the way of restoration of the old agrarian order; however, Agrarianism understood as a classical and Christian assertion of enduring values had not in any way become obsolete for Lytle. Nor had he abandoned his southern self-identity (his "knowledge carried to the heart"), though he had considerably complicated it by meditating on the perplexities of a backward-looking allegiance.

The stress of this position reflects the dialectical imagination, the quarrel with the self out of which, said William Butler Yeats, poetry is made. ("We make out of the quarrel with others, rhetoric, but of the quarrel with ourselves, poetry.")[14] In *A Name for Evil,* as in *The Velvet Horn,* Lytle shows his willingness to contemplate the dark side of reverence for tradition. This willingness is part of his dual consciousness, which is nourished by a vision of the old life yet starkly aware that the old life resides in the past. As Lytle implied in an essay written immediately after *A Name for Evil,* he was one of John Crowe Ransom's young friends "whose training contained the contradictions of their time" and who "more nearly represented the private sensibility before the spectacle of a breakdown in the common sensibility."[15] Out of this self-conscious awareness of his problematic relationship to his tradition, Lytle makes literature.

Despite the high hopes Lytle had for Cornsilk as a refuge against modern disorder, he decided that it did not obviate university work and related activities. Soon after the publication of *A Name for Evil,* he left with his family to teach writing at the University of Florida for twelve years. He then taught at the University of the South and edited the *Sewanee Review* for another twelve years, until retirement. Many circumstantial considera-

13. John M. Bradbury, *The Fugitives: A Critical Account* (Chapel Hill, 1958), 271.

14. William Butler Yeats, *Per Amica Silentia Lunae* (1917), in *Mythologies* (New York, 1959), 331. See also Allen Tate, "A Southern Mode of the Imagination," in *Collected Essays* (Denver, 1959).

15. Andrew Lytle, "Note on a Traditional Sensibility," in *Hero,* 174.

tions inevitably influenced the move, but one deep-seated reason Lytle left Cornsilk is suggested by a comment in *A Wake for the Living* about the farm's neighborhood. He writes that, when he bought the farm, "there was enough evidence that a rapidly changing society had not quite reached this area, but I didn't realize, what soon became clear, that we did not have a true community. My friends actually belonged to Nashville, and this part of Robertson County was for them a kind of private suburb." Thus, even at Cornsilk, the encroachment of the urban world and its frustration of "true community" were all too evident. Confronting the ubiquity of modernism both personally and artistically, Lytle judged regeneration of the past impossible. His experience at Cornsilk seems to have crystallized some important insights for him, apparent in *A Name for Evil.* In creating Henry Brent, Lytle became what he has said an artist should be: "a cannibal of Gargantuan appetite who does not exclude himself, if he is lucky." [16]

16. Lytle, *A Wake for the Living,* 262; Lytle, "The Working Novelist and the Mythmaking Process," in *Hero,* 192.

VIII

In the Inner Chamber
The Velvet Horn

> Like the poor the dead are always with us. They go unnoticed, but all along
> they await us in the inner chamber. And always it is a surprise. Oh, the impor-
> tunate presence . . .

His admired father having committed suicide, Lucius Cree is
forced to confront the importunate presence of his mother's, and
her three brothers', past. This is the situation in Lytle's last, best,
and most complex novel, published in 1957.[1] Daunting though it
is, and in movement winding and slow, *The Velvet Horn* in-
eluctably advances the reader into a world as intricately branched
as the deer antlers to which the title alludes. That this world
comes powerfully alive is partly owing to the compulsion with
which Lytle addressed his material. *The Velvet Horn* is Lytle's
most passionate work, its story having engaged his daemon more
intensely than any other in his career. Lytle has steadfastly put
into practice the doctrine of authorial effacement, but one none-

---

1. Andrew Lytle, *The Velvet Horn* (New York, 1957), hereinafter cited parenthetically by page number in the text.

theless senses the strong emotion that informed and drove this work in the nine years of its making.

Why does *The Velvet Horn* have this special intensity of tone, this seeming heightening of sensibility? Perhaps such matters must in the end remain mysterious, but some interesting conjectures arise from the testimony of Lytle's essay on the making of *The Velvet Horn,* "The Working Novelist and the Mythmaking Process."

In writing a historical novel set in the late nineteenth-century South, Lytle was turning to a world whose "ghostly presence" he had known in childhood, a society whose "last active expression," he has suggested, occurred sometime between 1880 and 1910. Yet the people whom this ghostliness surrounded were "alive in their entire being" and "seemed all the more alive because their culture was stricken."[2] Now entering his fifth decade and living in Gainesville, Florida, Lytle was far away in time and place from his home terrain—the southeastern margin of the Nashville Basin and the Cumberland hill country of Tennessee and Alabama—as it had been in his boyhood. But the places and the folk that had vanished now lived ever more intensely in his imagination. The writing of *The Velvet Horn* was thus a recovery, imaginatively, of a charged past and of the deepest strata of that world already disappearing when he was born.

One stratum was the hypertrophy of familial intimacy in the older South, which was "clearest in the country family, where the partial isolation meant an intimacy and constancy of association in work and play which induced excessive jealousy against intrusion from the outside." This jealous love "extended to the land and to natural objects with a possessiveness lasting even generations." Lytle has stated that he "did not have to look very far, no farther than both sides of [his] own house," for knowledge of such family introversion. Musing over his typewriter, he began to see this turning inward of the family circle as an "incest of the spirit," as "a spiritual condition which inhered within the family itself." This condition became the essence of the novel's subject.

2. Lytle, "The Working Novelist," in *Hero,* 178–79.

Incest, both spiritual and physical, took on a symbolic dimension suggesting forbidden yearning for prelapsarian wholeness, the destructive and futile impulse "to return to the prenatural equilibrium of innocence." Drawn partly from what Lytle divined of his ancestral world, the spiritual incest of the orphaned Cropleighs (and the physical incest of Julia and Duncan) unfolds its dark consequences in *The Velvet Horn.*[3]

That Lytle knew his ancestral world well is amply affirmed by his family memoir, *A Wake for the Living,* which provides an interesting gloss on *The Velvet Horn.* ("Shards," the chapter dealing with the Reconstruction era, is especially relevant.) An Uncle Peter, a Judge Ewing, an Aunt Nancy, who stepped down to marry a Mr. Tilford, and even a Widow Julia with her special friend, the squire (a "union man" who had made "a good deal of cash money by buying cotton and running it through the lines"), are among those mentioned in *A Wake for the Living* who are suggestive of characters in *The Velvet Horn.* Lytle's memory of his grandfather Nelson's black "Boswell" (his name, John Greer) contributed to the making of the novel's John Greer, Jack Cropleigh's manservant and companion. Through the transfiguring imagination, Lytle saw his memories anew and in a fuller light. As he states in *A Wake for the Living,* "A child doesn't think of adults as having lives of their own. They are fixtures in an unchanging world. A mother is a mother. A grandparent is old." Now he did think of these figures "as having lives of their own," and doing so was a spur to his imagination. Provocative possibilities emerged from behind the fleeting impressions of his childhood and the bare facts of family legend.[4]

Also emerging from remembrance was the look and smell and feel of the country itself—the red cotton fields in drought time, the snake-fenced turnpikes, the sour reek of the sawmill, the scrub pines and blackjack in abandoned farmland, the twisted laurel of the highland coves. When Lucius Cree pauses by the family fields to watch the spring plowing, he responds to the

---

3. *Ibid.,* 184.
4. Lytle, *A Wake for the Living,* 35, 200, 125, 199, 251, 211.

scene sensuously: the gees and haws of the plowboys come to him as "the oldest tongue"; "the dirt fall[s] back from the mold boards with the lift and curl of waves"; and the plunging mules are "like the heavy panting of the ground" itself (288). Lucius remembers how, in boyhood, he had wanted to plow, but his father had dissuaded him. "He had put it that you can't do it yourself and order it done: the hands will grow slack and careless, lose respect for you. 'I'm a good farmer,' his father had said, 'and I've never had a plow in my hands'" (290). The same conversation between Lytle and his own father is recorded in *A Wake for the Living.* The South's sense of family and place, Lytle has said, is what set it apart in America.[5] The degree to which he not only chronicles but shares that southern sense is reflected in the intense evocation of place in *The Velvet Horn.*

By immersing his imagination in the twilight world into which he had been born, Lytle was mining a rich lode for his fiction. In productive tension with his insistence on artistic objectivity and conscious craft—formal control in the tradition of Henry James and Gustave Flaubert—was the awakening of his daemon. The story's images seemed to spring from some subterranean fissure; in references to the book's creation, Lytle speaks repeatedly of mysterious promptings, of "intrusion from the depths." The concluding segment, he has said, was written in a virtual trance.

> As I drew toward the end, the last thirty pages or so, the artifice completely usurped my mind. It possessed me. There is no other word for it, and I've never quite felt it before. I became merely an instrument. . . . My impulse was to remain at the typewriter and not get up until the book was done, but this would be too long for my strength. Food and sleep were necessary, and the tactical considerations of how much changed from day to day. I could not bear to be touched or noticed. My nerves had drawn into the tissue of the skin. I forced myself to eat as in a dream. I would go to bed at seven or eight o'clock and rise each morning earlier, until I was getting up at two. In a kind of half-awareness I knew that I had to watch this expense of energy, or I would give out before the end. I

5. See *ibid.,* 35; Lytle, "The Working Novelist," in *Hero,* 179.

sensed that if I did, I would lose it, that once this possession of me by the actors was broken, it would never return.[6]

These "actors" compelling Lytle bore the spectral lineaments of his boyhood South. His memory of their prototypes, human beings who had been heightened and revealed against the backdrop of their stricken culture, must be considered among the chthonic sources prompting his imagination.

Memory is not only part of the inspiration of *The Velvet Horn* but also part of the technique. The interplay of past and present has concerned Lytle throughout his career. One thinks, for example, of the restive Agrarian in "The Backwoods Progression," for whom "tradition lodges in the blood."[7] Or, in the fiction, one thinks of young Dick McCowan at a crux in southern history; of Henry Brent and his nineteenth-century predecessor leaning across the generations in a sinister embrace; and more obliquely, of Hernando de Soto as the herald of modernism. Moreover, Lytle has frequently shown interest in the uses of a retrospective point of view, creating narrators who tell their stories from the dramatic platform of memory: MacGregor's son in "Mr. MacGregor," Kate McCowan with her stream-of-consciousness flashbacks in "Jericho, Jericho, Jericho," Pleasant and Lawrence McIvor in *The Long Night,* Henry Brent in *A Name for Evil.* Memory brings special effects and insights to each of these works, but in *The Velvet Horn,* it enters the fabric of Lytle's fiction with its greatest intensity and intricacy. Although Lawrence McIvor in *The Long Night* speaks of being "able to piece the story together" from his Uncle Pleasant's retrospective monologue and from what he "could learn from other sources," the actual process of piecing together is not a significant part of the book, as it is in *The Velvet Horn.*

The story line of *The Velvet Horn* progresses, as Lytle notes in "The Working Novelist and the Mythmaking Process," by "juxtaposition and accumulation rather than the steady advance of a

6. Lytle, "The Working Novelist," in *Hero,* 188, 191.
7. Lytle, "The Backwoods Progression," 430.

conflict." Emerging in partial revelations, oblique references, and revised hypotheses, the story is mediated through the perspectives of more than eight characters. Most of the narrative unfolds through the eyes of Jack Cropleigh and his nephew Lucius Cree, but Lytle filters parts of it through Sol Leatherbury (3–4, 373), Duncan Cropleigh (124–30), Hopgood Schott (147–59), Pete Legrand (160–78, 230–37, 313–24), Julia Cropleigh Cree (181–85), and Saul Slowns (264–72). There are also various brief interpolations of the thoughts and voices of others, as Lytle makes himself what he has called the "Hovering Bard." In his "Foreword to *A Novel, a Novella and Four Stories,*" he states, "Everybody in a country community knows something about a happening, but nobody knows it all. The bard, by hovering above the action, to see it all, collects the segments. In the end, in the way he fits the parts together, the one story will finally get told." A striking characteristic of "the way he fits the parts together" in *The Velvet Horn* is the novel's split-level time structure.[8]

The tension between the two parts of the time structure, which may be called the Cropleigh-past and the Lucius-present, makes possible much of the meaning and intensity of the novel. The skeleton of the present action involving Lucius is as follows. On the eve of his eighteenth birthday, Lucius goes to the mountains with his Uncle Jack, where he helps his uncle witch a well, has his first sexual experience, and then learns that his father, Joe Cree, has been killed by a falling tree. He returns to attend the funeral, faces the fact that his father's death was not an accident but suicide, and decides to continue the family's sawmill business with financial help from Pete Legrand. After hearing that he is Legrand's bastard (only his mother and Legrand, now that Joe Cree is dead, know he is more probably Duncan Cropleigh's bastard by incest), Lucius elopes with Ada Belle Rutter, the mountain girl who is pregnant with his child. Ada Belle's brother, thinking Lucius has merely run away with her, tries to shoot Lucius, but Jack steps in front of the bullet and is killed. At the

---

8. Lytle, "The Working Novelist," in *Hero,* 189, and "Foreword to *A Novel, a Novella and Four Stories,*" in *ibid.,* 200–201.

end of the story, Lucius is building a home with wood from the tree that killed Joe Cree.

The action of the Lucius-present does not by itself account for the peculiar power of *The Velvet Horn.* It is memory, Jack's in particular, that reveals the book's mythic understructure, the Cropleigh-past underlying the present action of 1879 and 1880. Jack remembers his parents' steamboat disaster, the fateful moments of the early lives of his brothers and sister, Legrand's disembowelment, Julia's wedding. Joe Cree (via Lucius) remembers the larger-than-life figures of the Civil War. Legrand remembers his passionate encounter with Julia in Parcher's Cove. Dickie Cropleigh remembers the fratricide-suicide of his brothers Beverly and Duncan. Julia remembers her night of incest. Furthermore, these remembered events have, in the mystery of time's passing, assumed an aura of legend. We sense that aura, for instance, when Lucius and Ada Belle stand on a ridge of the otherworldly Peaks of Laurel, surveying the moonlit woods below. She says "a man taken to the cove to live with the beasts, a time ago." And Lucius responds: "—Yes, I know. It was my Uncle Beverly" (228). Throughout the novel such legendary memories arise, and those who were once blindly caught in the toils of fate strain to find meaning in their memories. In sum, Lytle has his characters delve into the past both to reveal the presence of the "then" in the "now" and to unravel stories of mythic value.

In *The Velvet Horn,* an intricate piecing together of events precedes Lucius' discovery of his bastardy. At the outset of the story, Jack tells his nephew, "You think you are you . . . but when you came out of your mother's womb, you also came out of what happened to her and her brothers the day we learned our father and mother went up in fire and smoke" (12). The path of fate spirals between actions separated by decades. If the Cropleigh parents had not been killed in a steamboat explosion, then Beverly, the eldest son, would not have led his fellow orphans Duncan and Julia into the forest for a life of retreat. If they had not retreated, Julia would not have been oblivious of the saving restraints imposed by society on flawed human nature. If she had not been ignorant, she perhaps would not have gone with

Legrand into Parcher's Cove (or have been so vulnerable to incest with Duncan). If she had not lain with Legrand, casting her son's paternity in doubt, Joe Cree would not have committed suicide. If Cree had not committed suicide, Lucius would not have had to confront the tortuous mystery of his history. The radiations of fate from Julia and Legrand's night in the cedar grove are myriad, and they do not come to rest until Jack lies in his own blood.

Lytle shows, beyond a novelist's ordinary interest in cause and effect, a conspicuous interest in the weavings of fate, and so do his characters. Most good plots develop with a sense of narrative necessity, but this one is particularly complex, the characters themselves calling attention to that complexity. This elevates the act of piecing together history to a major theme of the novel. For Lucius and Jack, as well as for Lytle, history is of utmost importance and is not dead, static, or quaint. There is no idle memory in the unfolding of this story, no nostalgia—only the memory of what is making the present. We see, along with Lucius (indeed, more than Lucius), the inexorable march of events leading from the steamboat explosion that kills his grandparents to his own marriage to a mountain slattern—the end seeded in the beginning.

Uncle Jack, the central intelligence of the novel, broods repeatedly on the entanglements of present and past. Primarily through him, the interweavings of the time structure show how the past unfolds in Lucius' present and future. Jack both mediates and meditates the past, lamenting that Lucius has been "caught up at his coming to manhood" (101). But, despite Jack's urge to protect him, Lucius the boy, locked in "one blinding whirl of immediacy," must become Lucius the man, with a burgeoning sense of history (101). Indeed, the novel makes clear that Lucius' advent to maturity involves a deepening awareness of history.

Joe Cree's death opens the Pandora's box of the past, and Lucius soon discovers that history, as Jack says, is "the delayed surprise" (101). Jack, who immediately knows that Cree's death must have been suicide, now thinks, *Somebody told Joe Cree about that time, on the hunt, Julia and Pete Legrand got lost together"* (101). For Jack, Cree's suicide is the delayed surprise of Julia's night with Legrand nineteen years earlier. The delayed surprise in store for Lucius is the history of his birth, the knowledge that impelled his father to commit suicide. That the reader learns that history before Lucius does makes possible dramatic irony of the highest intensity.

Headed to the funeral in a buggy with Lucius, Jack falls into a reverie, tracing "the backward-stepping rocks" of memory's "dry stream bed . . . looking back to see forward" (101). The image of the past brings the present into perspective for him and for us. Riding down the old Indian trace, which Jack calls history's "path," he thinks, "Like the poor the dead are always with us. They go unnoticed, but all along they await us in the inner chamber. And always it is a surprise. Oh, the importunate presence . . ." (102). Besides Joe Cree, Jack is thinking of his dead brothers Duncan and Beverly, who have played a large part in the tragedy now unfolding. This is the onset of one of the book's many bold plunges back in time.

This plunge back to two decades earlier, through Jack's memory, constitutes almost all of the second chapter of the book. In it Beverly, disdaining the treadmill of the workaday world, chooses the wilderness sanctuary, Parcher's Cove, for his "fool's paradise" (110). The intense bond between Duncan and Julia, who also have grown up half-wild in the woods, is apparent. With the betrothal of Julia to Joe Cree, Duncan grows jealous and savage. Jack's memory turns to the events of the hunt on the day following the engagement announcement, when Julia and the newcomer Pete Legrand become separated from the rest of the party. Led by their brother Duncan, Jack and Dickie set out at twilight to find the couple. Beverly meets his brothers at the secret waterfall entrance to Parcher's Cove and leads them in, where at dawn they find Julia and Legrand sleeping by a dead fire. Duncan slashes Legrand's belly open in the ensuing knife fight. Dickie, a medical student, sews up his wound, plots a cover-up of the whole affair, and sends Julia back to camp with orders to marry Joe Cree right away. Beverly forbids anyone ever to return to Parcher's Cove.

As Jack emerges from his reveries, the image of his sorrowing nephew beside him blends with "that other image, that companion of another time, another journey," namely, Julia riding home with him from Parcher's Cove (142). This overlapping of images is strongly evocative, because Julia's actions long ago are what have brought Lucius to his present anguish. In a moment of keen dramatic irony, Lucius blames himself for his father's death: "It's my fault. . . . When I did it up there with that girl, I knew. I knew something bad would happen" (143). By means of Jack's memory, Lytle has brought us to greater knowledge than Lucius now possesses, thus heightening our sense of the pathos of his words and situation. Jack tells him, by indirection, what we would like to say and what Lytle has carefully prepared us to think: "The snarl of fatality. Who can pick its thread? Do you dip up water and find the source of the stream?" (143).

Later, at Cree's wake, Jack meditates further on the complications of history, in a passage near the heart of the novel's meaning.

> Unravel the past: weave the present. To what pattern? A pattern to keep Lucius from being undone by the knowledge this fresh death will bring up, for open the ground as you will the WAS jumps up as the NOW goes in and no time for the amenities. In and out, the two motions which make a whole but never are a whole. The old curse, division's sorrow, Duncan had tried to deny. Duncan and Beverly, each in his way. And where had it brought them all? Into the folded cove after the long hunt, to the spongy sod and rock, and like babes in the wood Julia sleeping in Pete Legrand's arms . . . this unraveling—he must break no thread. (201)

The old curse both Duncan and Beverly had tried to deny was original sin. Both had sought a prelapsarian world of changelessness and innocence, but "the garden they wandered was never there" (223). They are broken on the rack of this world because of all that the lure of paradise gulls them into defying: the division of the sexes, the inexorable process of time and change, man's flawed nature. As Lytle states, "This is an habitual impulse, the refusal to engage in the cooperating opposites that make life. It is also as illusory as any Golden Age, and forbidden by divine and human law." [9] Duncan cannot accept Julia's growth into womanhood, attempting to freeze his feelings in the "total innocence of love before carnal knowledge" (223). Beverly lives with the beasts in the fast-vanishing wilderness, renouncing his birthright in order to pursue a vision of Eden before Eve. Flux, however—the cooperating dimensions of "now" and "was"—rules this fallen world where "no act resolves itself of itself"; and in the end Duncan and Beverly die at each other's hands in a dynamite explosion at the entrance to Parcher's Cove (201). The moral is not lost on Lucius, for by the end of the novel, he has resisted many similar temptations to flee from his entanglement with life.

The juxtaposition of analogous tableaus from the present and the past is one of Lytle's most effective techniques for drawing the fullest meaning possible from his two-part time structure. The overlapping of images of Julia and Lucius in the buggy with Jack after related catastrophes is a function of Jack's memory. Earlier, the same merging occurs when Jack comes upon the sleeping figure of Lucius with news of Joe Cree's death. Seeing in Lucius' posture of lost innocence the figure of Julia in the grove nineteen years before, Jack thinks, "Is there only one image of fatality?" (95). The telescoping of images underscores not only that Lucius has duplicated his mother's sin by withdrawing into a secret place (another false Eden) and there taking Ada Belle, but also that, in archetypal terms, he, like his mother previously, is on the verge of receiving bitter knowledge and division after wholeness. Thus, repetition by analogy evokes the timelessness of certain events. [10]

On the second day of their marriage, Lucius and Ada Belle at Seven Springs call to the reader's mind an image much like that of Legrand and Julia upon first entering Parcher's Cove, "the world simple as the first day" (166). Like Legrand (and also like Beverly), Lucius is temporarily seduced by thoughts of "the still-

9. Lytle, "The Working Novelist," in *Hero*, 184.

10. On the novel's coherence in terms of archetype, see Thomas H. Landess, "Unity of Action in *The Velvet Horn*," in Bradford (ed.), *The Form Discovered*, 3–15.

ness of these woods, empty of humankind, wandering as through one eternal moment, unvexed by time" (351). But Lucius "knew better," and he resists the enticement of a false paradise—a treacherously sham immunity from culpability in the world of time—as Legrand did not (353).

The parallels of the two-part time structure show that Lucius comes to "know better" because he is immersed in history. He must look back to the traumatic events surrounding his conception in order to move forward in the present, for as Uncle Jack tells him, "choice don't take place in a vacuum" (363). Lucius' knowledge of his bastardy triggers his decision to marry Ada Belle. Mulling the past in conversation with Ada Belle, he comes to see his mother's coupling with Pete Legrand as akin to his own careless love of Ada Belle.

> He blurted out, "It's a treacherous blood. She fathered another man's child on father, on Captain Cree. My uncles too. Don't you see?" And then, "Who could know to look at her?"
>
> "A woman finds her man. Sometimes it's a sorrow." The voice was low and tender. "A woman will all the more keep his youngon from harm."
>
> "Do you think that's what she and Pete Legrand were thinking when they got me?"
>
> "No, I don't, Lucius."
>
> "Well, then."
>
> "Careless love don't think."
>
> The comparison stung him. (343)

And in a few moments the sting of the comparison intensifies, when he realizes that Ada Belle is about to marry another man in order to give her child a father. This confluence of the past and the present prompts Lucius to resolve that his child will "have his own father's name" (345). As Walter Sullivan points out, "At the end of the novel Lucius, having sought out the truth about his birth, assumes his own guilt which is inseparable from the guilt of his father. His atonement is private and sacramental, manifested in his marriage to Ada Belle."[11]

11. Walter Sullivan, *A Requiem for the Renascence* (Athens, Ga., 1976), xx.

The Velvet Horn illustrates that history, personal and public, shapes the present, burdening the poor player of this world with knowledge and mysteries with which he must come to terms. For Lytle, this coming to terms is a life-and-death matter. Lucius inherits the curse of ancestral crime and folly, which he must face squarely before he can come to a mature identity as an individual. When Lucius first learns he is a bastard, he becomes lost in self-pity and in a spurious sense of freedom, seeing himself as nameless and with "no inheritance to worry with" (332). When Lucius declares that he is planning to flee to the West, Uncle Jack delivers a lecture on the moral cowardice of flight, insisting that running away from the past is, in the end, running away from life. To run away is to disregard "all the conventions and institutions, everything that constrains the natural man and makes him aware of his neighbors, and so aware of himself and his peril" (358). Each generation must "grow out of" the history of the preceding one, as Jack well knows: "If you stay here, you and Ada Belle . . . you will know what your agony has brought you to and so try to handle it, and your child will be born into it and grow out of it into his own, which will not be yours but his own, and he will have a name in his own right" (362). But not until Jack steps in front of the bullet meant for Lucius does Lucius know with the heart's knowledge that "life was there, forsaken and forsaking" and "he could not flee it; only accept and bear it" (370). He determines to begin again, sawing up the tree that killed Captain Cree—which earlier he had been afraid to look at—for boards "to raise a small house to bring his wife to" (373).

Knowing the flaws and folly of the characters of the mythic backdrop, Jack is well qualified to coach Lucius past the pitfalls that have entrapped others. In the archetypal story of the Cropleigh children in the wilderness, Jack sees an eternal lesson, namely, that growing up brings sexual division, carnal knowledge, and awareness of time. That the world destroys those who deny these things is the meaning of the tale of the "brothers and sister, under the guidance of the eldest," who, as Lytle observes, "withdrew from the stresses of formal society in an effort to return to the prenatural equilibrium of innocence and wholeness."[12] As part of his beloved nephew's initiation into manhood, Jack tells Lucius all the essential parts of this tale except for Julia's fall from innocence, admonishing him, "Whatever the truth, put your eyes to it" (223). Jack's garrulity, the way he "talked around a thing, circumscribing it, as if he could make it show itself more clearly," is meant to save Lucius from repetition of the fatal mistakes of his forebears (11). Lucius, for his part, tries desperately to follow Jack's allusive talk, because he knows "his uncle never spoke idly" (53). After Jack has sacrificed his lifeblood, which leaves "a stain worth all the books," Lucius knows he has "Jack's words to stand on," forming a bridge across the past, as he accepts the flawed givens of his predicament (368, 373).

That Lucius does not easily accept guilt and human imperfection is not surprising, considering the powerful influence of Joe Cree. Lucius cherishes the memory of his father and at one point is intent on following in his footsteps; but eventually he develops a deeper understanding of life than Joe Cree, despite all the latter's admirable qualities, had been capable of. Lucius learns to live with the knowledge of evil, whereas Cree had been unable to reconcile it with his world view based on an abstract principle of honor. At the end of the novel, Lucius accepts the tragic outlook, akin to Job's, that his uncle and his experience had taught him. Cree, however, operated under a procrustean code of honor that turns out to be "a mighty lie" (153). The lumber inspector, Hopgood Schott, astonished that Cree had put him on his honor, and even more astonished that it works, observes, "There's nothing wrong with it. Only you've got no right to get people believing into thinking that's the way things are, that men can act out of honor in a daily way, that a man can always be a man, and then walk out and let a tree fall on you and mash people ten miles around. That's all that's wrong, to lie about the world and then run out on your lie" (152–53). Cree runs out on his lie when he learns that his supposed son is a bastard, possibly

12. Lytle, "The Working Novelist," in *Hero,* 184.

conceived in incest, and that the Cropleigh family, his kin, had dealt with him dishonorably in arranging his marriage. His rigid world view cracks under the strain of these revelations, and he kills himself by walking under a falling tree. (One remembers that he always strode through the woods oblivious to the snakes, that is, evil, underfoot.)

As Lucius' plight shows, taking on a spiritual inheritance can be a perilous task, for there are negative forces in our conceptions of the past that can be stumbling blocks for life in the present. Assuredly, memory can in certain respects be a stifling or morbid influence rather than a means to "that fuller knowledge which only the living past can give," as Lytle's depictions of Cousin Charles and Cousin Suds make clear.[13] Decadent, egg-sucking Charles, barely able to operate in the present, retreats from life's complexity into the simplicity of ancestral names on parchment. Despite Charles' obsession with the past, history has no meaning for him beyond the names of a genealogy. Indeed, the bloodlines of horses mean as much to him as those of people. Once he has hung Joe Cree's name onto the family tree, he observes, "Now he is safe. . . . Life. You never know, it's so . . . but here they hang in unbroken line" (217). The person who would confront the meaning of the past will not find it, as Jack says to Lucius, "in the dead wood of all those genealogical trees" (195).

Cousin Suds, unable to accept that he has been ruined by General Sherman's march, determines to defy Sherman's boast that "he would bring every southern woman to the washboard" (220). Obsessed by a symbol of the past life, he ruins his nine daughters' hands to keep his wife's soft. Suds's adherence to a vision of the antebellum South is a distortion of the historical sense and blinds him to the exigencies of change and defeat. As Jack says, "A hand does all the things it was made to do. What Suds picks up is that thing he's put behind his sight. Put there in the terror of the truth" (221). And even while Jack is telling his nephew this story, the time is quickly approaching when Lucius

13. Lytle, *A Wake for the Living,* 4.

must have no terror of the truth. Suds and Charles fail where Lucius eventually prevails—in nerve and judgment.

Lytle's technique of balancing "then" against "now" gives force to his portrayal of the changes in society that demand Lucius' nerve and judgment. The private events of the novel are part of a public pattern, and the broad historical currents of the enveloping action are subtly depicted. Indeed, Lytle's depiction of the South at a historic moment of tension between the traditional and the modern strikingly reveals—to quote Allen Tate speaking of the Southern Renascence generally—"the peculiarly historical consciousness of the Southern writer." This historical consciousness, Tate says, empowered "the curious burst of intelligence" the South experienced at its "crossing of the ways." [14]

The "crossing" apparent in Tate and Lytle's time had its origins, to judge from *The Velvet Horn,* in the previous century. Lucius comes of age in a culture stricken and passing into its dark corridor of change. ("And Appomattox has more to do with it than you think," says Jack Cropleigh [54].) Lucius' South, *circa* 1880, is at "the effective turning point of the great revolution which was to diminish a Christian inheritance," Lytle has said, disclosing his particular myth of the South. That myth, Robert Weston has explained, pictures the Confederacy's defeat as "another in the long line of defeats since the Renaissance of the sacred order, and perhaps the ultimate example in modern times of the triumph of the secular, materialistic, 'Faustian' world view." Lytle began to formulate this Spenglerian outlook in the days of Agrarian campaigning. In 1933, in "The Backwoods Progression," for instance, he deplored the chaos of values released into the modern world by "the moral revolution that changed the mediaeval concept of the economic commodity from the thing-to-be-used to the thing-to-be-sold," and portrayed the South as Western civilization's last venue for the ill-starred

14. Allen Tate, "The Profession of Letters in the South," in *On the Limits of Poetry* (New York, 1948), 281.

struggle of the agrarian state of mind against middle-class materialism and impiety.[15]

Lucius is a member of a defeated society, and as Lytle has said, "the defeated are self-conscious. They hold to the traditional ways, since these ways not only tell them what they are but tell them with a fresh sense of themselves. Only defeat can do this. It is this very self-consciousness which makes for the sharpened contemplation of self. . . . The sudden illumination made life fuller and keener, as it made life tragic. But it stopped action." [16] This keen but tragic contemplation of self one especially sees in Jack Cropleigh, whiskey prophet of *The Velvet Horn,* whose keeping of the homeplace, as his brother Dickie discerns, has deprived him of a home (213–14). The chaos of Jack's farm office—seed catalogs, broken hames, double shovel points, cotton samples flung helter-skelter in all the disorder of "abandonment"—is perhaps a sign of "stopped action," of cultural arrest (354). The sight strikes Lucius "with all the violence of a spiritual vertigo" (354). Another sign is the Cree mansion, still unfinished over a decade and a half after its construction was interrupted by the Civil War. Inside the columns, the house is a shell, its rooms unplastered and skeletal. Joe Cree "would finish it right or not at all," but for Julia it is "like living in the hollow of a skull" (186, 297). Erected from Cree's dynastic impulse ("who must have seen it as himself lasting in the brick, the future forecaught in the dwelling that would house his heir"), the house will never hold his heir (186). Indeed, it is not the traditional but the modern man, Legrand, who will finish it.

In Lytle's portrayal, traditional southern culture gradually became, after the war, as much a shell as Captain Cree's house. Its manners and mores took on a brittle rigidity as, defeated in arms, the South sensed but resisted the defeat of its ethos as well. Seeing the cycles of history in "circling spiral," Lytle viewed the

15. Lytle, "The Working Novelist," in *Hero,* 179; Robert V. Weston, "Faulkner and Lytle: Two Modes of Southern Fiction," *Southern Review,* n.s., XV (1979), 39; Lytle, "The Backwoods Progression," 413.

16. Lytle, "The Working Novelist," in *Hero,* 183.

South through a revealing lens. What was left of the culture's life force, Lytle has said, "remained in the surface forms. . . . The shed skin for a while shines with life, but the force of life is already on its night sea journey." The gradual withdrawal of cultural forces first reveals itself, Lytle divined, "in the hardening of traditional laws and forms, foreshadowing rigidity: that is, death." [17] To finish the house "right," for Captain Cree, would be to finish it after the grand antebellum manner, now an abstract pattern. Trapped as he is in desperate postwar realities, his rigid and doomed insistence is symptomatic of "the hardening of traditional laws and forms."

Grotesques that they are, Suds and Charles provide the book's most distinct examples of the hardening of conventions in a moribund society. Sherman's march, Jack tells Lucius, "ruined Suds. Complete. House gone, barn, stock, tools, slaves. Nothing but the land left, with no fence to tell its lines, the dirt of one field running into the next around the world. That's too far to see. It's an ailment as old as the common cold, the terror of the distant view" (221). The traditional way of life that had been everything to him suddenly destroyed, Cousin Suds is confronted with the "chaos" that, as Lytle has written, "is the underlying condition of any artifice" such as the family or the state. [18] Because he cannot face this elemental state of being, he concentrates every vanished feature of the old order into the image of his wife's lily hands, a virtual icon. In his "terror of the distant view," he cannot look into the glare of truth: fenced acres, "grateful" slaves, and white-handed belles do not exist by imperishable decree. The way of life that kept a lady's hands white has made its forced exit, but Suds, with his "literal mind" and obsession with a "surface form," still insists, "One southern lady won't soil her hands" (200).

Cousin Charles betrays an apposite case of cultural agoraphobia. His genteel preoccupation with the family pedigree is a re-

17. *Ibid,* 182–83.
18. *Ibid,* 183.

flection of Old South traditionalism. His room staled by the egg-shell pile rising three feet high, old Charles keeps the line of the Crees and their Lindsay Arabians. Genealogy, for him, holds the brittle iconic value that Molly's white hands hold for Suds. Abstracted from flesh and blood beings, the inked-in names hang from the limbs of the family tree in sterile, bathetic tribute to family continuity and the dynastic idea of the "house." Charles' desiccated obsession suggests the very rigor mortis of traditional forms. That he is the sacred scroll's guardian is indication enough that the line is played out, that the force of life is on its "night sea journey" elsewhere.

In view of the reason for Captain Cree's suicide, it is ironic that as Lucius leaves his old cousin's room on the eve of the wake, Charles is murmuring, "Now, boy, for your own branch" (217). Almost certainly the issue of Duncan Cropleigh (as Charles might well phrase it), Lucius has no branch in the Cree genealogy. The Old South's insistence on womanly purity, Lytle has suggested, "was not chivalric romanticism but a matter of family integrity, with the very practical aim of keeping the blood lines sure and the inheritance meaningful." [19] Joe Cree's recoil at the revelation of his wife's impurity, then, is from a blow not only heart shattering but code shattering as well; it is a shock not only personal but in a sense social, too, striking at the core of his family-centered traditionalism.

Cree's response, outraged rejection of Julia and then suicide, shows him related to Suds and Charles in more than blood. A small detail from the wake provides a clue: Lucius confuses the smell of his father's corpse, laid out in the parlor's August heat, with that of Cousin Charles.

As he looked, he almost said aloud—Why, he's fat . . . and then it curled into his nostrils, thick and lazy; it struck his stomach like a blow. What's Cousin Charles doing in here, he thought, and looked behind, and there was nobody but his mother and uncles, then Rhears lifting the top and in his hands it seemed as light and thin as

19. Lytle, "Foreword to *A Novel, a Novella and Four Stories,*" in *Hero,* 200.

an eggshell. Those eggshells . . . he fled and heard his mother's voice, stifled, "Lucius"

there on the porch, with the bitter acrid taste in his mouth, his stomach heaving, he said, no, no, he looks like this. But not his father's face but the features of his Cousin Charles instead to mock him. (215)

How can Captain Cree—in many ways the most attractive character in the novel, a compelling, duty-loving Augustus—be at all analogous to Cousin Charles? The answer is related to the issue of cultural stasis, the "hardening of traditional laws and forms, foreshadowing . . . death."

Cree's pride and honor have become rigid. Told by Duncan's vindictive widow that Lucius is Legrand's child, Cree rushes into his wife's sewing room. Yet he "stood somewhere way off," Julia remembers, "not where he was," that is, he becomes abstract, in a sense, transformed into a materialization of principle. He demands, *"Is it true, woman?"* and in the word *woman,* from this man "ever perfect in courtesy," Julia as a person is negated, along with nearly two decades of marriage. Julia says: "I tried to tell him, to say—Does all our life long together mean nothing to you? . . . But nothing I could do or say could unfreeze that look of shocked righteousness" (318). He sees a blackened symbol now, not Julia, and whether he ever saw Julia apart from her symbolic value is uncertain. This man, "whose life was the care and the increase and the just government of his inheritance," cannot forgive the transgressions against honor and purity that shake the cold iron of the inherited code underlying his material patrimony (114).

He has become "righteousness . . . hard as stone," which "never melts in love," Julia sees. He had never loved her, she intuits, but had only put her "into the pieces of his mind." The "puzzle," though, "was all scattered," she tells Legrand. "That's what his face told me, puzzle pieces put together with paste, all in the wrong places. Gashes of white paste" (319). The game metaphor is revealing, suggesting well the abstract, artificial, rule-conscious kernel of Cree's character, which has made symbolic game pieces, in a sense, of wife and son. There is truth in Julia's cry, *"Marbles in your head that click and click. And the taw your wife, and the taw your son you knocked out of the ring"* (319). The lowly Luke Nobles seems willing, out of love, to accept a child who is not his own and a wife who is not a virgin. Joe Cree is unwilling, even for the sake of eighteen years of father and son affection. He will not even "say one word out of pity" or try to understand the vulnerable fourteen-year-old child that Julia was when she conceived Lucius (320). The matter, for him, involves the transgression of fundamental tribal rules and cannot be privately resolved one sorrowing human to another. Years before, Jack Cropleigh had realized "that if Joe Cree ever doubted, he was damned" (114). The moment of doubt, after nineteen years, has come. Cree is "the good son, the just master, the upright citizen, the kinsman who knew a kinsman's dues," and he performs his duties with "a simplicity of belief which makes all action swift and sure and a world with only the minimum of complication" (17, 18). But such simplicity, Jack knows, only "serves up to a point," which Joe Cree is forced beyond (18).

Suds Pilcher must have his dove-white lady, Cousin Charles his ancestors "in unbroken line," and even Nate Rutter his boiled shirt. And Joe Cree must have his family circle, that core element of southern culture, as pure as snow, with clear title all around. In the self-consciousness of southern defeat, Cree clings righteously to the brittle husk of the traditional ways. With the "puzzle pieces" of his idea (wife, estate, heir) coming unglued, he commits suicide. No more than Cousin Suds can he bear to look into, and come to terms with, the chaos underlying the conventions of his stricken culture. His inherited blueprint in tatters, he orders the tree "the whole country locates itself by" cut down, then walks under it as it falls (147). The old order's landmarks are doomed, he seems to say; I shall go with them. The towering oak that crushes him is called the "boundary tree," and it might be said to mark the boundary between the traditional and the modern (371).

All about Lucius lie signs of the disintegration of the Cumberland hills' version (quoting Lytle) "of the older and more civilized America, which as well retained the pattern of its European inheritance." [20] From both outside and inside the old order is embattled, from the lumber agent's "belief that the means did not matter" to shifts even in the boss-and-worker compact at the Cree sawmill (see 159, 278–79, 287). The debasement of traditional values, for instance, is both pathetic and monstrous when, at the novel's end, the vulgar Ada Rutter moves down from the mountains into the former house of Lucius' relatives. There she apes respectability, marrying off her formerly promiscuous daughters, "getting" religion, and starving her invalid husband to death so that she can advance up the social and material scale through remarriage. Furthermore, Beverly, as the firstborn Cropleigh, should represent the landed stability of the family, but he abdicates traditional responsibility. Eventually, the Cropleigh family dissolves—in Jack's words, "all scattered, and scattered our common love" (15). Duncan and Beverly die at each other's hands; Jack and Dickie remain unmarried and childless. The Cree family, also among the country's homegrown patricians, comes to a similar pass when Joe Cree, the spokesman for family and community values, and "the balance wheel in this county," commits suicide (192). While the agrarian order is eroding, the newcomer Legrand prospers. Outsider, moneylender, shrewd gin and mill owner, he is symbolized by his ledgers. His motto is, "The hand that gives is above the hand that receives" (178).

Figurations of the clash of two conflicting world views abound, and the new one, which exalts material ends as the only reward for action, gains ascendance. Joe Cree valorously heads an irregular outfit in "his own private little war" against the northern invaders, and he astounds small-time swindlers like Hopgood Schott by putting them on their honor (151). In contrast, Legrand the modern, "such a man as multiplied," makes his fortune during the Civil War by selling contraband cotton to the North (110). To compare Schott's "Like any man I take what I

20. Lytle, "The Working Novelist," in *Hero,* 178.

can get" with Cree's "Everything, even a board, has its true value" is to see plainly the opposition of expedience and higher principle (147, 151). When thrown into confusion by Cree's code of honor, Schott goes for confession, in a sense, to the materialist priest Legrand. The "secret, flour-screened office," Lytle writes, "the office of commerce, had taken on a formal privacy beyond its function" (152). With Cree dead now, Schott presents himself to Legrand not primarily to make a business proposition but "to be restored to the belief that the means did not matter, the end was all" (159). With Legrand, he is sure, business is "strictly business" (147). (Schott does not know he has approached Legrand on the one matter, involving Julia, that is *not* strictly business.)

In sharpest antithesis to the forces of expedience and materialism is Jack Cropleigh, who heroically sacrifices his life for Lucius. Just minutes before he falls to Othel Rutter's bullet, Jack tells his embittered nephew, "God said before the world was, I am. And somewhere in Proverbs, that love is a divine play. Brought to earth, it's a mighty rough game and no holds barred. That's the game you are called on to play, son, and win or lose, it's for keeps. But not here, or so we are told. You play here, but the score is settled elsewhere. And then it ceases being a game" (362). In contrast, Legrand in the end can only say to his stepson, "Money can help. I'm always behind you" (372).

This opposition of cultural forces is far from schematically drawn, however. A collision of values is part of the enveloping action, but the characters are not etched in the blunt outlines of mere historical exemplars. Pete Legrand is a case in point. He is a hard and willful man who knows, as he says, "the way to do business for a profit": Stay on the lonesome turnpike, remain impersonal, and "never talk to a man in the fields or in his house about business" (175). When his one friend, the Yankee outsider Slowns, asks, "Where does the hand of love lie?" Legrand replies, "Where I put it" (178). Such hubris bespeaks not only Legrand's private deficiency but Lytle's somber view of Western history as well. Legrand is an avatar of that juggernaut of the world drama, the will-dominated modern, and as such has kindred in the "wealth-warrior" of "The Hind Tit," the "modern Prometheus" of "The Backwoods Progression," de Soto in *At the Moon's Inn*, and even Henry Brent in *A Name for Evil*.

However, Legrand, like de Soto and Brent, is much more than a representative of a type. He is not in reality a passionless villain who intends to snatch a widow's property, as those at the wake think, nor is he, at the novel's end, any longer a disciple of the will. In love with Julia since he first saw her, Legrand for nineteen years has been "like a man called out of his bridal night to go some far distance" (319). The ache of his scar is real, and it triggers the memory that has marked him forever—his riding into Parcher's Cove with Julia and then, in the cedar grove, the bearskin blanket sliding off her shoulders.

In the years' empty interim he has waited and watched, amassing his wealth, whispering behind clenched teeth, "my wife, my son." He becomes a "passionate husk," this man whose guts were cut out. His hoarding and waiting have "bought empty days and years," yet he hones himself on his creed that the unrelenting will is all (thus he feels contempt for the weak-willed who devote themselves to drinking, whoring, restlessly moving on, or buying what they cannot afford) (172). When a flood washes away his grist mill and gin, though, Legrand is shown that "the hand that gives" is not his own but, as Rhears says while pulling Legrand himself out of the current, "old Marster's" (314). Baptized into a new awareness by the floodwaters and by fresh sorrows, he knows, by the story's end, how little the raw will (and money, its vehicle) can accomplish the things that most matter. He does gain Julia, but she is suddenly aged and heartsick. And, in the home he has longed for, "nobody can claim kin"; he can never know if Lucius is his son (247).

That Legrand should be presented in human, not schematic, dimensions is part of Lytle's aesthetic. "You do not write about a society living or dead," Lytle has said. "You write about people." A crucial moment in the composition of *The Velvet Horn*, Lytle has suggested, occurred when the characters began to assert autonomy, that is, the "moment . . . when the actors in the stress of the situation will come 'alive,' will make a response that reveals them." Nonetheless, to bring his characters to life, Lytle had recourse to "a restraint as conventional as blank verse," location. "People do not live in a vacuum," Lytle observes. "They live somewhere. . . . The natural man is an abstraction. He has never been seen, but what is natural to men always shows itself shaped by the manners and mores, the institutional restraints, of a given time and place." [21]

The time and place of *The Velvet Horn*—the particular tastes and proprieties, customs and conventions, estates and classes, shifts and stresses of the upper south at a pivot in history—are carefully drawn. Lytle is writing not about a society but about individuals "who live within the constraint of some inherited social agreement." This is the resolution of the paradox: the unique men and women caught up in history represent the universal "men and women caught in some one of the human predicaments forever repeating themselves." [22]

Lytle has said the germinating impulse of *The Velvet Horn* was "to resuscitate a dead society," the later nineteenth-century South. As the work progressed, however, the historical and conceptual element of a dead society was absorbed within a deepening field of vision. Lytle had begun reading in archetypal psychology—in Carl Gustav Jung's *Psychology and Alchemy,* Erich Neumann's *The Origins and History of Consciousness,* Heinrich Zimmer's *The King and the Corpse*—and a deep interest in the mythic patterns of human experience became part of the conscious craft of *The Velvet Horn.* It "came" to him, Lytle further states, "that it is the archetypes which forever recur; are immortal, timeless; it is only the shapes in which these appear that seem to harden and die, that is, the manners and mores that are unique to a given society, and these shapes are the appearances of reality, the world's illusion moving within the illusion of time."

21. *Ibid,* 182, 181, and "Foreword to *A Novel, a Novella and Four Stories,*" in *Hero,* 198.
22. Lytle, "The Working Novelist," in *Hero,* 182, and "Foreword to *A Novel, a Novella and Four Stories,*" in *Ibid.,* 195.

Thus, beneath the surface of temporal history—the manners and mores of Tennessee and Alabama hill country, *circa* 1880—is another reality, that of myth and archetype. The falling oak that crushed Captain Cree may be said to mark not only the boundary between the old and the new South but also a mythic boundary. Called "the seed tree of the world," existing "from the time of man," the "line tree" marks the border of Eden, for *The Velvet Horn* retells an "ancient drama" (Lytle's words), "the state Adam and Eve found themselves in after Eve had been taken from Adam's side" (149, 3). The boundary tree is thus an example of the way *The Velvet Horn* operates simultaneously on planes historical and archetypal. Similarly, Lucius can be said to have made two journeys in the course of the novel, one within "the illusion of time" and the other beyond time. He is part of the historical flattening of southern society—the leveling of class hierarchies—as he makes his "night sea journey" from being Joe Cree's heir to being no one's, and he merges with immemorial myth as he journeys from childhood to maturity, as he experiences his "fall" into the human condition ("the same old song, Paradise lost and the world gained" [195]).[23]

In retracing the growth of his interest in "the archetypes which forever recur," Lytle chronicles his realization that any particular culture, from this Olympian point of view, is merely "the world's illusion moving within the illusion of time." Then he makes the arresting statement, "What a shock this was to my partial and emotional view of the South!" Seeing the South even within the context of Western history since the Middle Ages did not now seem altogether enough. It was to be seen within the sweep of "the circling spiral of change" since the beginning of

23. Lytle, "The Working Novelist," in *Hero,* 181, 179, 182, 187, 183. For discussions of the novel's mythic, archetypal elements, see Anne Foata, "La Leçon des Ténèbres: The Edenic Quest and Its Christian Solution in Andrew Lytle's *The Velvet Horn,*" *Southern Literary Journal,* XVI (1983), 71–95; Landess, "Unity of Action in *The Velvet Horn,*" in Bradford (ed.), *The Form Discovered,* 3–15; Clinton W. Trowbridge, "The Word Made Flesh: Andrew Lytle's *The Velvet Horn,*" *Critique,* X (1967–68), 53–68; and Weston, "Faulkner and Lytle: Two Modes of Southern Fiction," 34–51.

civilization. Indeed, comparing the South's history to "the cycles which other societies go through" and, in particular, the traditional South's decline to the decline of other cultures, Lytle began to see in southern history an archetypal pattern—the night sea journey of the force of life, "the repetitive thrust out of chaos into the surrounding void." Lytle implies that, at the outset of the novel's composition, he had perhaps been too concerned with his southern characters *as* southerners because of his own feeling for the manners and mores of the traditional South.[24]

Against the backdrop of what is timeless in the human drama, however, Lytle began to brood on the inescapable mutability of any culture's particular set of manners and mores. His attitude became very like that recommended to Lucius by Jack Cropleigh, in his story of an Indian manhood ritual.

The Indian boy was always put down among the women, but the time came when they drove a stick through the fleshy part of his chest, tied thongs at each end and from there to the pole, and all day long leaning back to keep the thong tight, with head back and eyes open to the sun, he followed it blazing about the pole. And in the West there are no trees or clouds to block the view. . . . But if he made the circle, the boy died but the man was there. And afterwards the horizon did not seem the promise or terror of space, nor did he see in the seasons the grind of time but in both that eternal reflection, for he had seen the circle come back on itself, and that great distance the sun come down to the eye . . . forever drowned in that illumination which is all. That's why the Indian's eye is clear and steady. (221–22).

The Indian has had a vision of the eternal, and thus he neither fears nor craves what lies beyond the horizon of his own place and time. He is neither in flight from his tradition nor narrowly obsessed with it. Time, he sees, is not linear but, like the horizon, a "circle come back on itself." Lytle's eye had become similarly clear and steady as he tried consciously to see through a place and time to the universal. As he remarks in the opening words of

24. Lytle, "The Working Novelist," in *Hero,* 183–84.

A Wake for the Living, he had "come to live in the sense of eternity." [25]

Lytle did not, however, try to strip *The Velvet Horn* of its southernness, for he believed that in historical fiction "the author must first absorb the period of his scene so thoroughly that the accidental restraints of manners and customs become the medium of representation of what is constant in human behavior." Indeed, in the context of a discussion of *War and Peace,* Lytle has claimed for the historical novel a special double ability to reveal the meaning of a particular era and, if ambitious, of "all time." In fiction that "assumes the past," writes Lytle, "you have not only the illusion of the present, but the past permeates the immediacy of this illusion; the fictive personalities take on a certain clairvoyance; the action a double meaning, as if the actors while performing disclose the essential meaning of their time, even of all time." [26] Lytle assayed this merging of the historical and the archetypal in *The Velvet Horn.* Thus, for instance, the novel's Aunt Amelie, widowed Daughter of the Confederacy and image of the old life's blighting, is as well the agent of the gods' will in a mythopoeic drama (vide the marble Mercury above her secretary). And thus the tangled matter of Lucius' paternity, considered symbolically, is quite meaningful. Born into a culture in upheaval, Lucius is, as a historical symbol, the child of both the old and the new, both Cree and Legrand. This is the paradox he can never escape (361). On the mythic level, the mystery of his genesis allows him to be seen, in even deeper focus, as the cursed result of the perennial desire for forbidden wholeness, the son of the brother and sister who "walked the woods in that careless joy before the world began" (320).

The Velvet Horn is more than a southern story of a family among families in a time of cultural stress. Lytle recognized that however much he might regret the passing of the old communal life of place and role—and define himself in relation to that pass-

25. Lytle, *A Wake for the Living,* 3.

26. Andrew Lytle, "Caroline Gordon and the Historic Image," in *Hero,* 155, and "The Image as Guide to Meaning in the Historical Novel," in *Hero,* 8.

ing—southern experience was not, by itself, the center of his field of vision. He knew and loved the traditional South of his father and grandfathers, and as an artist he drew on that love and knowledge. Yet his artistic focus was not simply on the old things that passed away and what displaced them but also on the ancient things that stay the same. The dead who "await us in the inner chamber" speak, in this novel, in accents both southern and universal.

IX

Agrarian Coda
A Wake for the Living

The radiations of fate between past and present, and the tension between the traditional and the modern, are relevant to a consideration not only of *The Velvet Horn* but also of Andrew Lytle's life. To bring up Lytle's life in a discussion of *A Wake for the Living,* published in 1975, may at first seem digressive, for despite its being a book of family anecdotes, *A Wake for the Living* hardly includes Lytle at all; he appears as little more than an observer in most of the stories, often observing at the remove of a century or two. Yet the book is more about Lytle than one might suppose; indeed, it is perhaps more about him than an autobiographical discussion of his literary friendships and his own exploits would have been. In describing the ancestral life from which his life evolved, Lytle reveals significant things about the circumstances of time and place that made him an artist and about the continuity of his Agrarian thought over forty-five years.

Written, as Lytle says, to tell his daughters who they are and where they come from, *A Wake for the Living* chronicles the family history of Nelsons and Lytles from colonial days ("In a Far Country") to the modern South as late as 1942 ("The Land of Nod"). Although he does not specifically discuss the telling of stories, Lytle nonetheless makes abundantly clear that he and his daughters come from a storytelling culture. Through humor, a rich assortment of characters, and casual tale-telling, *A Wake for the Living* bodies forth the southern folk imagination in delightfully concrete fashion. There are the many anecdotes, for instance, involving lovelorn and alcoholic Uncle Jack—for example, his comment on Cousin Ada's fart as she bends over surreptitiously to pinch a flea under her skirts: "That's right, Ada. If you cain't ketch him, shoot him." [1] Or there is the story, handed down through the generations, of an eighteenth-century Lytle named Micajah, "a legend in the family of the hard-bitten life of the frontier."

> He came into the world a-bouncing. He was stout as a mule colt and hard as a pine knot. He didn't want his mother to wean him. Her sister advised with her, and they decided to mix a potion of lard and quinine and cayenne pepper, grease her nipples with it. That surely would break him of the need, as he was going along to be a big boy. One evening by sun he bounced in and squared himself. "Mammy, let me have it," he said.
> "Here 'tis, son. Come git it."
> He took it and jumped back like a snake had bitten him. He turned to his father. "Pappy, give me a chaw of tobacco. Mammy's been eating bitterweed." (83)

A Wake for the Living brims with such stories, most of them obviously uttered by other family tongues first. That Robert Lytle, Andrew's father, was in his time an applauded hearthside raconteur shows the potential Antaean connection between an artist and his regional soil. Caroline Gordon muses on this connection in a letter to Andrew Lytle in 1943, shortly after the elder Lytle's death.

> I was impressed by the fact that on his [Robert Lytle's] last visit here he solved for me a technical problem that might have held me up for days, weeks. That is, there were some difficult problems of timing involved in that chapter. . . . I felt that Mr. Lytle's stories

---

1. Andrew Lytle, *A Wake for the Living: A Family Chronicle* (New York, 1975), 215, hereinafter cited parenthetically by page number in the text.

about Sawney Webb did the trick better than anything I could ever have thought up for myself and I have felt very grateful to him for supplying them just when they were needed.

Which leads me to reflect on his story-telling gift. He was an artist. I remember his other story about crowning your mother with the watermelon halo, and I remember thinking at the time that it came to him just as it would have come to an artist, waking him up in the night, he said. He knew it was good!

Thinking of the Lytle family's "mute, inglorious Miltons" in the background behind Andrew, Gordon continues: "The traits that go to make up the artist, like those that make up Nietzsche's Superman, are a long time in the making. Some ancestor who was himself a frustrated artist perfected that gift of story telling to the point where he could use it. The roots of his talents often lie beneath the level of his own consciousness but he is all the stronger for that." Further back, beyond the elder Lytle, Gordon concludes: "there are others that I don't know about. But I think you have enough of the power derived from them (and I am sure that it is a tremendous part of the artist's power) coupled with your own great and original talent to push you inevitably forward." [2]

In retelling the tales of *A Wake for the Living*, and no doubt adding his own embellishments, Lytle reveals his roots in a folk tradition, rural and communal in character. That it can be, and has been, a fertile tradition for the would-be artist might best be suggested by adding to Caroline Gordon's remarks the words of a participant in a similar literary renascence across the Atlantic. As Irishman William Butler Yeats said to his countryman James Joyce:

The artist, when he has lived for a long time in his own mind with the example of other artists as deliberate as himself, gets into a world of ideas pure and simple. He becomes very highly individualized and at last by sheer pursuit of perfection becomes sterile. Folk imagination on the other hand creates endless images of

2. Caroline Gordon to Lytle, March 15, 1943, in Lytle Papers.

which there are no ideas. Its stories . . . are successions of pictures like those seen by children in the fire. . . . In the towns . . . you don't find what old writers used to call the people; you find instead a few highly cultivated, highly perfected individual lives, and great multitudes who imitate them and cheapen them. You find, too, . . . an impulse towards creation which grows gradually weaker and weaker. In the country . . . you find people who are hardly individualized to any great extent. They live through the same round of duty and they think about life and death as their fathers have told them, but in speech, in the telling of tales, in all that has to do with the play of imagery, they have an endless abundance. . . . Everything seems possible to them, and because they can never be surprised, they imagine the most surprising things.[3]

Even more germane than what Yeats says about the fecundating power of the "folk imagination" is the dynamic of antithetical forces that his remarks imply. In the background behind Yeats's distinction between folk imagination and the sterile urban imagination is Ireland's rapid shift in Yeats's time from an agrarian to an urban-industrial society—a shift that left him standing with one foot in each world. In the American South, Andrew Lytle also stood with one foot in each world, finding himself, like Dick McCowan in "Jericho, Jericho, Jericho" and Lucius Cree in *The Velvet Horn,* at the confluence of the old and the new. The period of his youth, the first part of the twentieth century, was, Lytle writes, "a historic moment everywhere in the Western world. . . . It was the last moment of equilibrium. . . . For almost overnight, with the automobile for symbol of the change, the community disappeared." To come of age at this pivotal "historic moment" was a fermenting circumstance for a young southerner and fledgling writer like Lytle. This scion of a storytelling tradition was, in a sense, nagged into literary art by his aggravated awareness of change and his Janus-faced vision of past and present. Especially in dramatizing Lytle's sense of living in a time of upheaval, *A Wake for the Living* bears out his remark in 1974 that what he is "really saying" in his family chronicle is, "This is

3. Quoted in Richard Ellmann, *James Joyce* (New York, 1959), 107.

the life which makes an artist, which unconsciously prepared me to be a writer."[4]

A deeply elegiac passage from *A Wake for the Living* well illustrates the way in which the book shadows forth the conditions that made Lytle a writer. The passage involves Lytle's memory of a day, sometime in the late 1920s or early 1930s, when he makes a trek to see what once had been his great-grandfather's house outside Murfreesboro. The front door stands ajar, open not only to "winds and weather" but, as Lytle's description steadily underscores, to time itself. "The long hall held the empty silence of a grim hospitality. In places the French block wallpaper hung in strips, showing the heavy plaster behind. It was the color of tobacco juice with threads of hog hair all twisted through it. The hair kept the plaster from cracking. At first I thought the tiny black curlicues were worms" (253–54). Walking past fluted columns and climbing to the empty third-floor ballroom, Lytle imagines "the gallop and swing" of old dances and the "sweet and sour odors of the heated bodies." The old life of the place suggests itself as well in the Civil War tunnels that honeycomb the ground below the lower hall. Along the staircase, upon whose papered walls images are discernible, he moves, in a sense, through history—past medieval "hunters eating their collops of deer" and then past eighteenth-century "English men and women riding elegantly," the red fox just ahead. Finally, again outside in the sunlight, he casts a look behind him and suddenly feels "the ruin that had overtaken all that this dwelling had held" (255).

Lytle says casually that he left the house with "no ghosts following." One might well say the ghosts did not need to follow, for the man who later wrote *The Velvet Horn* and *A Wake for the Living* himself contained them, in the same way that Quentin Compson of Faulkner's *Absalom, Absalom!* is "a barracks filled

4. Lytle, "Note on a Traditional Sensibility," in *Hero,* 173, and interview with Anne Foata, Fall, 1974, in Anne Foata, "Andrew Lytle et le Mythe Edenique" (Ph.D. dissertation, Université des Sciences Humaines de Strasbourg, Institut d'Etudes Anglaises et Nord Americaines, 1981), 825.

with stubborn back-looking ghosts" and "an empty hall echoing with sonorous defeated names." Like young Quentin, Lytle is the son of one world, the older, communal South, and yet the inhabitant of another, the twentieth-century South. Thus Lytle shares the "peculiarly historical consciousness" (to quote Tate) of the southern literary renascence generally, which produced, in addition to *The Velvet Horn,* many another work deeply marked by the vectors of change in the modern South: Faulkner's *Absalom, Absalom!,* Thomas Wolfe's *Look Homeward, Angel,* Robert Penn Warren's *All the King's Men,* Eudora Welty's *The Golden Apples,* Tate's "Ode to the Confederate Dead," and on the list goes. As small and understated a story as it is, Lytle's dramatized memory of walking through the ruin of his ancestor's house nevertheless reveals a man at the South's "crossing of the ways," too intensely aware of the currents of time and change in his culture to remain one of its mute, inglorious Miltons.[5]

The degree to which the ultimate terms of Agrarianism have remained alive for Lytle is readily apparent in *A Wake for the Living.* Lytle's post-1930s Agrarian career took a path midway between those of his friends Ransom and Davidson. In the 1940s, as Louis Rubin has shown, Ransom retreated from the Agrarian allegiance while Davidson, by contrast, clung to Agrarianism so devotedly that he "was ever willing to bend literature to extraliterary needs." As for Lytle, at no time in his later career does he repudiate the inheritance he figuratively acceded to in *Bedford Forrest* and fiercely defended in *I'll Take My Stand.* His attitude toward the southern past becomes considerably more complicated as he shifts his energies from polemics to literature, but he does not disavow Agrarianism as did Ransom. Yet neither does he take Davidson's virtually propagandistic tack. (Indeed, along with Tate and Ransom, Lytle put himself at far enough a philosophical distance from Davidson that Davidson noticed.) The broad purport of Agrarianism remains alive to Lytle, but it in-

5. William Faulkner, *Absalom, Absalom!* (New York, 1936), 12; Tate, "The Profession of Letters in the South," in *On the Limits of Poetry,* 281.

volves no program for reviving a vanished society, no reductive adherence to a party line. Lytle has been protected by his aesthetic from overly simple southern partisanships that might otherwise have adulterated his fiction. "It should be obvious that polemics is one discipline and fiction another," Lytle writes. "If you are going to preach, get into the pulpit; it you want to bring about political reforms, run for office; social reforms, behave yourself and mind your manners. . . . When a novel obviously makes an appeal other than its proper aesthetic one, you may be sure it has been written with the left hand."[6] Lytle's art has deep roots in southern experience, but few of its pages have been written with the left hand of the narrow partisan. It is literature in the service not of a South-defending dogma but of "felt life."

A Wake for the Living is nevertheless suffused with Lytle's still-abiding Agrarian convictions. Many of the anecdotes embody Agrarian sentiments, such as Lytle's story of Mrs. Tucker, the descendant of a venerable Virginia family, at one of the southern watering places in the old days.

> Mrs. Bishop Tucker was taking the waters at White Sulphur, and one morning after breakfast was rocking on the verandah. Nearby several young women, overdressed and loud of speech, were bemoaning a mishap to an acquaintance of theirs. The husband had bought a farm and was forcing his wife to live on it with him. This seemed to the women plain tyranny. Mrs. Tucker turned to them and said mildly that farm life was not all that unpleasant. Indeed she herself had been born on a farm. There came a pause, as the ladies examined too closely her simple but impeccable attire. All civility, however, had not deserted them. "And where was that?" one of them asked.
>
> "Mount Vernon," she replied. (242–43)

Herein, figuratively, is a gentle reprimand from George Washington himself to those contemptuous of the "provincial" countryside.

6. Rubin, *The Wary Fugitives,* 288–89, 262; Davidson to Tate, February 23, 1940, in Fain and Young (eds.), *Literary Correspondence,* 324; Lytle, "Foreword to *A Novel, a Novella and Four Stories,*" in *Hero,* 194.

There are passages in *A Wake for the Living* that speak in far less gentle tones. When meditating the American Indians' belief in magic, Lytle writes: "One wonders, is magic indigenous to the world we took from the Indians? Is our economy of profane possession more proficient in its technology? Will our magical belief in matter as the only value not bring us to a disaster as final as the Indians received? Will we then imitate the stake and electrocute the scientist and the engineer for our common failure to make all substance give up the secret, and for our particular impiety in substituting the laboratory for the altar?" (53). In "The Hind Tit," nearly half a century earlier, Lytle had spoken in similar terms of science versus the Word. "Seek a priesthood," he had advised, "that may manifest the will and intelligence to renounce science and search out the Word in the authorities."[7]

Further, the domestic parallel to the altar is the hearth, and in "The Hind Tit" and the other early essays, Lytle had returned again and again to the fundamental value of attachment to family and place. *A Wake for the Living* shows no slackening of this belief. Musing on his great-grandfather's will, for instance, Lytle pauses to make the following thoroughly Agrarian statement: "He knew that nothing like farmlands, kept together, each division being contiguous to the one next to it, would sustain the sense of kinship. His children would know well and be sustained by fixity to place. Climate and the knowledge of a small area, learned each day and season, would protect and make them scholars of nature. Fast travel, too dramatic and changing a geography, dazzles the eye and loses the man through ignorance" (160). As "scholars of nature," these descendants would learn, in the words of "The Hind Tit," "nature's invincible and inscrutable ways," which instruct man in his limitations and thus prevent him from brutalizing either nature or himself.[8]

The image of Lytle studying a will has a symbolic aptness, for the very act of seeing the present in the light of the past remains at the heart of his southernness. As he observes in *A Wake for the*

7. Lytle, "The Hind Tit," in *I'll Take My Stand,* 244.
8. *Ibid.,* 228.

Living: "If we dismiss the past as dead and not as a country of the living which our eyes are unable to see, as we cannot see a foreign country but know it is there, then we are likely to become servile. Living as we will be in a lesser sense of ourselves, lacking that fuller knowledge which only the living past can give, it will be so easy to submit to pressure and receive what is already ours as a boon from authority" (4). Throughout the thirties—in *Bedford Forrest,* in "The Backwoods Progression"—Lytle, along with his Agrarian brothers, had responded to precisely this concern. Looking to the "living past" of his region, he had formulated a sense of man's place in creation that the typical American, obsessed with the future and with materialism, had lost. Tradition, said Lytle in his essay on John Taylor, is a force against "natural chaos always a-pounding upon the doors of society."[9] *A Wake for the Living* bears the same message, as its epigraph from Yeats signals:

> How but in custom and in ceremony
> Are innocence and beauty born?
> Ceremony's a name for the rich horn,
> And custom for the spreading laurel tree.

Reverence for family, place, tradition, and the things of the spirit is evident in both *I'll Take My Stand* and *A Wake for the Living,* despite the passing of nearly half a century between the two works, suggesting the continuity of Lytle's Agrarianism. To be sure, the "crusading spirit" Davidson noted in the Lytle of 1932 was long gone by 1975, as well it might be. The Agrarian battle, on the economic plane at least, had been decisively lost, and Agrarianism as a group undertaking had been dead since the late 1930s. Images from Lytle's own family experience—Cornsilk Farm under TVA waters, a shopping center spreading its asphalt where his great-grandfather's cedar forest had once stood—help explain the change in mood from crusade to wake (see 259, 255). But on a higher plane the ideas behind Lytle's Agrarianism,

9. Lytle, "John Taylor and the Political Economy of Agriculture," IV, 99.

then and now, have hardly shed their chastening significance. In a way, they are the ideas behind the other epigraph of *A Wake for the Living,* the words of Isaiah, another man who failed to turn his nation from idolatry: "Thou hast multiplied the nation, and not increased the joy: they joy before thee according to the joy in harvest, and as men rejoice when they divide the spoil." [10]

10. Isa. 9:3.

Selected Bibliography

Works by Andrew Lytle

BOOKS

Alchemy. Winston-Salem, 1979.
At the Moon's Inn. New York, 1941.
Bedford Forrest and His Critter Company. New York, 1931.
Ed. *Craft and Vision: The Best Fiction from "The Sewanee Review."* New York, 1971.
The Hero with the Private Parts: Essays by Andrew Lytle. Foreword by Allen Tate. Baton Rouge, 1966.
The Long Night. New York, 1936.
A Name for Evil. New York, 1947.
A Novel, a Novella and Four Stories. New York, 1958.
Stories: Alchemy and Others. Sewanee, 1984.
The Velvet Horn. New York, 1957; rpr. Sewanee, 1983.
A Wake for the Living: A Family Chronicle. New York, 1975.

SHORT STORIES

"Alchemy." *Kenyon Review,* IV (1942), 273–327.
"The Guide." *Sewanee Review,* LIII (1945), 362–87.
"Jericho, Jericho, Jericho." *Southern Review,* 1st ser., I (1936), 753–64.
"Mister McGregor." *Virginia Quarterly Review,* XI (1935), 218–27.

"Old Scratch in the Valley." *Virginia Quarterly Review,* VIII (1932), 237–46.

ESSAYS AND REVIEWS

"Afterword: A Semi-Centennial." In *Why the South Will Survive,* by Fifteen Southerners. Athens, Ga., 1981.

"Agee's Letters to Father Flye." *Sewanee Review,* LXXI (1963), 164–65.

"The Agrarians Today: A Symposium." *Shenandoah,* III (Summer, 1952), 30–32.

"Allen Tate and John Peale Bishop." *Grand Street,* II (1982), 148–56.

"Allen Tate: Upon the Occasion of His Sixtieth Birthday." *Sewanee Review,* LXVII (1959), 542–44.

"The Approach of the Southern Writer to His Material." Atlanta *Constitution,* November 29, 1936, Book Sec., 14.

"At Heaven's Gate." *Sewanee Review,* LI (1943), 599–602.

"The Backwoods Progression." *American Review,* I (1933), 409–34.

"Caroline Gordon and the Historic Image." *Sewanee Review,* LVII (1949), 560–86.

"The Displaced Family." *Sewanee Review,* LXVI (1958), 115–31.

"Follow the Furies." *Southern Review,* 1st ser., I (1935), 203–205.

"The Forest of the South." *Critique,* I (Winter, 1956), 3–9.

Foreword to *The South, Old and New Frontiers: Selected Essays of Frank Lawrence Owsley,* edited by Harriet Chappell Owsley. Athens, Ga., 1969.

"A Hero and the Doctrinaires of Defeat." *Georgia Review,* X (1956), 453–67.

"The Hind Tit." In *I'll Take My Stand: The South and the Agrarian Tradition,* by Twelve Southerners. New York, 1930; rpr. Baton Rouge, 1977.

"How Many Miles to Babylon?" In *Southern Renascence: The Literature of the Modern South,* edited by Louis D. Rubin, Jr., and Robert D. Jacobs. Baltimore, 1953.

"The Image as Guide to Meaning in the Historical Novel." *Sewanee Review,* LXI (1953), 408–26.

"Impressionism, the Ego, and the First Person." *Daedalus,* XCII (1963), 281–96.

"In Defense of a Passionate and Incorruptible Heart." *Sewanee Review,* LXXIII (1965), 593–615.

"John C. Calhoun." *Southern Review,* 1st. ser., III (1938), 510–30.

"John Taylor and the Political Economy of Agriculture." *American Re-*

view, III (Sept., 1934), 432–37, III (Oct., 1934), 630–43, and IV (Nov., 1934), 84–99.

"A Journey South." *Kentucky Review,* I (1980), 3–10.

"Lee's Lieutenants." *Sewanee Review,* LI (1943), 177–79.

"Life in the Cotton Belt." *New Republic,* June 3, 1931, pp. 77–78.

"The Lincoln Myth." *Virginia Quarterly Review,* VII (1931), 620–26.

"*A Moveable Feast:* The Going To and Fro." *Sewanee Review,* LXXIII (1965), 339–43.

"Note on a Traditional Sensibility." *Sewanee Review,* LVI (1948), 370–73.

"The Old Country Store." *Southern Folklore Quarterly,* XVIII (1954), 246–47.

"A Partial Reading of Parade's End; or, the Hero as an Old Furniture Dealer." In *The Presence of Ford Madox Ford: A Memorial Volume of Essays, Poems, and Memoirs,* edited by Sondra J. Stang. Philadelphia, 1981.

"The Passion of Alex Maury." *New Republic,* January 2, 1935, pp. 227–28.

"Principles of Secession." *Hound and Horn,* V (1932), 687–93.

"The Quality of the South." *National Review,* March 8, 1958, pp. 236–37.

"R. E. Lee." *Southern Review,* 1st ser., I (1935), 411–22.

"A Reading of Joyce's 'The Dead.'" *Sewanee Review,* LXXVII (1969), 193–216.

"Regeneration for the Man." *Sewanee Review,* LVII (1949), 120–27.

"The Search for Order in American Society: The Southern Response." *Southern Partisan,* II (Fall, 1981), 21–24, 29.

"The Small Farm Secures the State." In *Who Owns America?,* edited by Herbert Agar and Allen Tate. Boston, 1936.

"The Son of Man: He Will Prevail." *Sewanee Review,* LXIII (1955), 114–37.

"The State of Letters in a Time of Disorder." *Sewanee Review,* LXXIX (1971), 477–97.

"A Summing Up." *Shenandoah,* VI (Summer, 1955), 28–36.

A Tactical Blunder." *Virginia Quarterly Review,* IX (1933), 300–303.

"They Took Their Stand: The Agrarian View After Fifty Years." *Modern Age,* XXIV (1980), 115–19.

"The Town: Helen's Last Stand." *Sewanee Review,* LXV (1957), 475–84.

"The Working Novelist and the Mythmaking Process." *Daedalus,* LXXXVIII (1959), 326–38.

Unpublished Correspondence

Letters from Andrew Lytle to:
> Davidson, Donald, February 21, 1929, November 2, 1932. Donald Davidson Papers. Special Collections, The Jean and Alexander Heard Library, Vanderbilt University.
>
> Owsley, Frank Lawrence, October, 1936, March 23, 1939. Frank Lawrence Owsley Papers. Special Collections, The Jean and Alexander Heard Library, Vanderbilt University.
>
> Tate, Allen, January 31 and November 26, 1929, Spring, 1930, June, 1930, February 23 and May 21, 1933, October 18, 1943, January 18, May 13, and October 16, 1944, July 8, 1947. Allen Tate Papers, Box 28. Princeton University Library.

Letters to Andrew Lytle from:
> Davidson, Donald, June 11, 1929, February 3, 1930. Andrew Lytle Papers. Special Collections, The Jean and Alexander Heard Library, Vanderbilt University.
>
> Gordon, Caroline, March 15, 1943. Andrew Lytle Papers.
>
> Owsley, Frank Lawrence, October 3, 1936. Andrew Lytle Papers.
>
> Ransom, John Crowe, December 11, 1925. Andrew Lytle Papers.
>
> Tate, Allen, March 15, 1927, April 1 and July 31, 1929, June 9, 1930. Andrew Lytle Papers.

Works on Andrew Lytle

BIBLIOGRAPHICAL

Kramer, Victor A. *et al. Andrew Lytle, Walker Percy, Peter Taylor: A Reference Guide.* Boston, 1983.

Polk, Noel. "Andrew Nelson Lytle: A Bibliography of His Writings." *Mississippi Quarterly,* XXIII (1970), 435–91.

Wright, Stuart. *Andrew Nelson Lytle: A Bibliography, 1920–1982.* Sewanee, 1982.

CRITICAL

Amacher, A. W. "Myths and Consequences: Calhoun and Some Nashville Agrarians." *South Atlantic Quarterly,* LIX (1960), 251–64.

Benson, Robert G. "The Progress of Hernando de Soto in Andrew Lytle's *At the Moon's Inn." Georgia Review,* XXVII (1973), 232–44.

Bradbury, John M. *The Fugitives: A Critical Account.* Chapel Hill, 1958.

Bradford, M. E. "The Fiction of Andrew Lytle." *Mississippi Quarterly,* XXIII (1970), 347–48.

———, ed. *The Form Discovered: Essays on the Achievement of Andrew Lytle.* Jackson, Miss., 1973.

———. "Toward a Dark Shape: Lytle's 'Alchemy' and the Conquest of the New World." *Mississippi Quarterly,* XXIII (1970), 407–14.

Carlson, Thomas M. "A Reading of Andrew Lytle's *The Velvet Horn.*" *Southern Review,* n.s., XXII (Jan., 1986), 15–36.

Carter, Thomas H. "Andrew Lytle." In *South: Modern Southern Literature in Its Cultural Setting,* edited by Louis D. Rubin, Jr., and Robert D. Jacobs. Garden City, 1961.

Clark, Charles C. "The Fiction of Andrew Lytle: From Old Scratch's Cannibal World to Paradise." *Occasional Review,* II (1974), 127–52.

———. "*A Name for Evil:* A Search for Order." *Mississippi Quarterly,* XXIII (1970), 371–82.

Cook, Martha E. "The Artistry of *I'll Take My Stand.*" *Mississippi Quarterly,* XXXIII (1980), 425–32.

Core, George. "A Mirror for Fiction: The Criticism of Andrew Lytle." *Georgia Review,* XXII (1968), 208–21.

Couch, W. T. "The Agrarian Romance." *South Atlantic Quarterly,* XXXVI (1937), 419–30.

Cowan, Louise. *The Fugitive Group: A Literary History.* Baton Rouge, 1959.

———. *The Southern Critics.* Irving, Tex., 1971.

Davidson, Donald. "*I'll Take My Stand:* A History." *American Review,* V (1935), 301–21.

———. *Southern Writers in the Modern World.* Athens, Ga., 1958.

De Bellis, Jack. "Andrew Lytle's *A Name for Evil:* A Transformation of *The Turn of the Screw.*" *Critique,* VIII (Spring, 1966), 26–40.

———. "The Southern Universe and the Counter-Renascence." *Southern Review,* n.s., IV (1968), 471–81.

Fain, John Tyree. "Segments of Southern Renaissance." *South Atlantic Bulletin,* XXXVI (May, 1971), 23–31.

Foata, Anne. "Andrew Lytle et le Mythe Edenique." Ph.D. dissertation, Université des Sciences Humaines de Strasbourg, Institut d'Etudes Anglaises et Nord Americaines, 1981.

———. "Andrew Lytle's *The Velvet Horn:* A Hermeneutic Approach to Wholeness." *Mississippi Quarterly* XXXVII (Fall, 1984), 429–53.

———. "La Leçon des Ténèbres: The Edenic Quest and Its Christian Solution in Andrew Lytle's *The Velvet Horn*." *Southern Literary Journal*, XVI (1983), 71–95.

Ghiselin, Brewster. "Trial of Light." *Sewanee Review*, LXV (1957), 657–65.

Gray, Richard. *The Literature of Memory: Modern Writers of the American South*. Baltimore, 1977.

Hesseltine, W. B. "Look Away, Dixie." *Sewanee Review*, XXXIX (1931), 97–103.

Hoffman, Fredcrick J. *The Art of Southern Fiction: A Study of Some Modern Novelists*. Carbondale, 1967.

Inge, M. Thomas. "The Continuing Relevance of *I'll Take My Stand*." *Mississippi Quarterly*, XXXIII (1980), 445–60.

Jones, Madison. "A Look at 'Mister McGregor.'" *Mississippi Quarterly*, XXIII (1970), 363–70.

Karanikas, Alexander. *Tillers of a Myth: Southern Agrarians as Social and Literary Critics*. Madison, Wis., 1966.

Krickel, Edward. "The Whole and the Parts: Initiation in 'The Mahogany Frame.'" *Mississippi Quarterly*, XXIII (1970), 391–405.

Landess, Thomas H. "Unity of Action in *The Velvet Horn*." *Mississippi Quarterly*, XXIII (1970), 349–61.

Landman, Sidney J. "The Walls of Mortality." *Mississippi Quarterly*, XXIII (1970), 415–23.

MacKethan, Lucinda H. *The Dream of Arcady: Place and Time in Southern Literature*. Baton Rouge, 1980.

———. "*I'll Take My Stand*: The Relevance of the Agrarian Vision." *Virginia Quarterly Review*, LVI (1980), 577–95.

Mencken, H. L. "Uprising in the Confederacy." *American Mercury*, XXII (1931), 379–81.

O'Brien, Michael. *The Idea of the American South, 1920–1941*. Baltimore, 1979.

Paschall, Douglas. "A Foreword to Andrew Lytle." *Ploughshares*, IX (1983), 196–201.

Purdy, Rob Roy, ed. *Fugitives' Reunion: Conversations at Vanderbilt, May 3–5, 1956*. Nashville, 1959.

Ransom, John Crowe. "Fiction Harvest." *Southern Review*, 1st ser., II (1936), 399–418.

Rock, Virginia J. "The Making and Meaning of *I'll Take My Stand*: A Study in Utopian-Conservatism, 1925–1939." Ph.D. dissertation, University of Minnesota, 1961.

Rubin, Louis D., Jr. *The Faraway Country: Writers of the Modern South.* Seattle, 1963.

———. Introduction to the Library of Southern Civilization edition and introduction to the Torchbook edition, *I'll Take My Stand: The South and the Agrarian Tradition,* by Twelve Southerners. Baton Rouge, 1977.

———. *The Wary Fugitives: Four Poets and the South.* Baton Rouge, 1978.

Simpson, Lewis P. "Andrew Lytle: Artist and Critic." *Southern Review,* n.d., XIX (1983), 833–35.

———. *The Dispossessed Garden: Pastoral and History in Southern Literature.* Athens, Ga., 1975.

Singal, Daniel Joseph. *The War Within: From Victorian to Modernist Thought in the South, 1919–1945.* Chapel Hill, 1982.

Stewart, John Lincoln. *The Burden of Time: The Fugitives and Agrarians.* Princeton, N.J., 1965.

Sullivan, Walter. *A Requiem for the Renascence.* Athens, Ga., 1976.

———. "Southern Novelists and the Civil War." In *Southern Renascence: The Literature of the Modern South,* edited by Louis D. Rubin, Jr., and Robert D. Jacobs. Baltimore, 1953.

Tate, Allen. Foreword to *The Hero with the Private Parts: Essays by Andrew Lytle.* Baton Rouge, 1966.

———. "A Prodigal Novel of Pioneer Alabama." *Books,* September 6, 1936, p. 3.

———. "The Profession of Letters in the South." In *On the Limits of Poetry.* New York, 1948.

———. "A Southern Mode of the Imagination." In *Collected Essays.* Denver, 1959.

Trowbridge, Clinton W. "The Word Made Flesh: Andrew Lytle's *The Velvet Horn.*" *Critique,* X (1967–68), 53–68.

Warren, Robert Penn. "Andrew Lytle's *The Long Night*: A Rediscovery." *Southern Review,* n.s., VII (1971), 130–39.

Weatherby, H. L. "The Quality of Richness: Observations on Andrew Lytle's *The Long Night.*" *Mississippi Quarterly,* XXIII (1970), 383–90.

Weston, Robert V. "Andrew Lytle's Fiction: A Traditional View." Ph.D. dissertation, Stanford University, 1972.

———. "Faulkner and Lytle: Two Modes of Southern Fiction." *Southern Review,* n.s., XV (1979), 34–51.

————. "Toward a Total Reading of Fiction: The Essays of Andrew Lytle." *Mississippi Quarterly,* XXIII (1970), 425–33.

Woodward, C. Vann. *The Burden of Southern History.* Rev. ed. Baton Rouge, 1968.

Young, Thomas Daniel. *The Past in the Present: A Thematic Study of Modern Southern Fiction.* Baton Rouge, 1981.

Yow, John. "Alchemical Captains: Andrew Lytle's Tales of the Conquistadors." *Southern Literary Journal,* XIV (1982), 39–48.

Index

Absalom, Absalom! (Faulkner), 138–39

Agar, Herbert, 38

Agrarianism: leaders of, 16; beginnings of, 17; meaning of, 30–32; as social program, 34–35; essay-reviews by Lytle on, 38–39; Lytle's role in, 38; values inherent in, 43–44, 89; religious element, 47; dissipation of, 50; in "Jericho, Jericho, Jericho," 57–58; *At the Moon's Inn* and, 85–89; and modern evils, 86–87; Lytle's changing view of, 102–103, 139–40; in *A Wake for the Living,* 139–43

Agriculture: idealization of, 23, 28; industrialization of, 24, 26, 28–29; return to rural life, 101–102. *See also* Farmers

All the King's Men (Warren), 139

American Democrat, The (Cooper), 33

American Indians, 79–80, 83–84, 141

American Review, 39, 47

American Revolution, 41–42

"American Scholar, The" (Emerson), 33

At the Moon's Inn (Lytle): willful pride, 47, 52, 79, 81–89, 128; summary, 77–78; materialism as theme, 78–79, 85, 88; sensuality as spiritual suicide, 79–81; wilderness imagery, 79–80; Christian chivalry in, 81, 88; religion in, 81–84; violence in, 83; moon imagery, 84–85; moral dimension, 87–89; tension between values in, 88–89; rape in, 95

Backwoods pioneer, 40–41

"Backwoods Progression, The" (Lytle): South's link with medieval world, 39–40, 43–44, 46, 47, 87–88; original publishing plans, 39*n*–40*n*; image of backwoods pioneer, 40–41; cultural decay, 44–46; nature of human imperfectibility, 46–47; religion in, 47; theme, 51; modernism in, 86; Agrarian themes, 100, 142; willful pride, 128